TRAGICOMEDY AND
CULTU

£4.95

EDINBURGH STUDIES IN CULTURE AND SOCIETY

General Editors: John Orr and Colin Nicholson

John Herdman
THE DOUBLE IN NINETEENTH-CENTURY FICTION

David McCrone and Brian Elliott
PROPERTY AND POWER IN A CITY: The Sociological
  Significance of Landlordism

John Orr
TRAGICOMEDY AND CONTEMPORARY CULTURE: Play and
  Peformance from Beckett to Shepard
TRAGIC DRAMA AND MODERN SOCIETY: A Sociology of
  Dramatic Form from 1880 to the Present
TRAGIC REALISM AND MODERN SOCIETY: The Passionate
  Political in the Modern Novel

Stanley Raffel
PLEASURE, VALUE AND FRIENDSHIP IN HABERMAS AND
  POST-MODERNISM

Tragicomedy and Contemporary Culture

Play and Performance from Beckett to Shepard

John Orr

Reader in Sociology
University of Edinburgh

MACMILLAN

First published 1991

Published by
MACMILLAN ACADEMIC AND PROFESSIONAL LTD
Houndmills, Basingstoke, Hampshire RG21 2XS
and London
Companies and representatives
throughout the world

Filmset by Wearside Tradespools,
Fulwell, Sunderland

Printed in Hong Kong

British Library Cataloguing in Publication data
Orr, John 1943–
Tragicomedy and contemporary culture: play and performance from Beckett
to Shepard.
I. Title
822.91409

ISBN 0–333–44879–0 (hardcover)
ISBN 0–333–53697–5 (paperback)

Contents

Acknowledgements

I would like to thank Ruby Cohn, Dragan Klaic, Dan Gerould, Randall Stevenson and Olga Taxidou for their many helpful comments and suggestions during the writing of this book. For better or worse, the finished product is entirely mine.

Edinburgh

JOHN ORR

1
Modernism and Tragicomedy

This book is concerned with tragicomedy as part of the modernist turn in the twentieth century. The word 'tragicomedy' is used consciously and deliberately by Beckett as a description of *Waiting for Godot*. But definition of it is elusive. In its modern context it signals the final breakdown of the classical separation of high and low styles. In *Godot* the comic waiting of Didi and Gogo is just as important as Pozzo's tragic reversal of fortune. Equally tragicomedy is a departure from the realist dramas of bourgeois conscience. It is, by contrast, a drama which is short, frail, explosive and bewildering. It balances comic repetition against tragic downfall. It demonstrates the coexistence of amusement and pity, terror and laughter. But it also delineates a new dramatic form which, from Pirandello onwards, calls into question the conventions of the theatre itself. The modernist turn and the admixture of tragic and comic elements, the sudden switch from darkness to laughter, or vice versa, come together in a twofold challenge. We are confronted with a world in which there appears to be little continuity of character or of action. We are never sure whether people or events referred to in dramatic speech have any objective validity. We never know as an audience how we are meant to identify physical landmarks or characters with peremptory names. Things just happen. Other things may never have happened at all.

This book argues that there is a structure to this apparent confusion, a historical development which starts with Pirandello and moves through Beckett and Genet to the plays of Pinter and Shepard. It entails a complex transformation in, to use Raymond Williams's term, structures of feeling.[1] Above all, it is a movement away from a sense of social experience anchored in tangible issues of moral right, of the good and the just and of their betrayal. Initially it is part of a general response to the crisis in value and the collapse of order in European society from 1910 to 1925 through war, revolution and economic catastrophe. Modernism, that elu-

1

sive label for a heterogeneity of contrary artistic movements, fractures experience and at its best makes it as uncertain as the theory of relativity had made our knowledge of cosmic nature. The structures of feeling I have discerned in tragicomedy, and which I shall discuss in due course, play and disremembering – or disrecognition – are responses to major uncertainties on all planes of knowledge. They move away from the constituent features of modern tragedy up to that point, those complex feelings of entrapment by unjust practices which provoke reversal of fortune and ruin the individual life. That is to say, they depart radically from modern tragedy's most liberal formulation, those agonising dilemmas of conscience its vulnerable heroes cannot resolve.

Moreover, as modern heroes lack more and more the sources of wealth and power, as they move down the social order, their tragic stature also starts to diminish. Tragic experience which resonates with wider social loss in addition to deep injustice, as in Ibsen, becomes weak if it degenerates into a purely local experience of the unjust. John Gabriel Borkman and Hedda Gabler are tragic figures precisely because they abuse power as well as being power's victims. They are accustomed to wealth and to status. They inflict as well as receive injury on a grand scale. With Ibsen's compressed and oblique use of the past they are given a previous life which is a resource for their power and its subsequent nemesis. The heroes of tragicomedy from Beckett onwards have no such resources. They have little wealth, few possessions and no cultural capital. Their lives are lived in a state of bewilderment as if they are playing out a game whose rules they did not invent and do not understand, a game that none of them can win. It is not their character or their personality which betrays them. It is their status and their predicament. They are largely nobodies in an unknowable world. Even where they are somebody, as they often are in Genet, their power in the world is an illusion and works only if others believe in that illusion too.

Modern tragicomedy challenges above all Ibsen's belief in the dramatic illusion of reality. In Pirandello the hollow nature of theatricality is turned into a modernist device at the same time as it was being turned into a political device by the leader of his country whom Pirandello then supported, Benito Mussolini. If Mussolini made the political arena echo with the amplified sound of his hollow boasting, stage-managed as an intoxicating spectacle for the modern crowd, Pirandello turned the pure theatricality of the stage into a nightmare, a living hell from which there seemed no escape. In his plays the pain of the presentation of self in any form is all too evident. His characters desperately want to perform in order to communicate who they are and what they feel, but when they perform they no longer know who they are, only that they are no longer themselves. Performance instals itself between what they are forced to be and what they consider to be their true selves. Their nature and their personas part company. The only possible reconciliation of the two is for them to believe in the illusion they have created. Our sense of what human nature is, and how the theatrical persona 'represents' it, is called brutally into question. Already we have the Beckettian predicament in its embryonic form: the way in which performance traps its protagonists into a series of endless and cyclical 'plays' on their own existence when they have no idea what the status of their existence actually is.

It is this vital, latter point which separates Pirandello from Chekhov. The uncertainties of Chekhov's pre-revolutionary world can be defined in terms of clear social landmarks. Ennui and superfluity are structures of feeling which infect the provincial country house. But within this collective malaise the social and psychological differences of the characters are still telling ones, and they are still surrounded by the paraphernalia of familiar objects. The future is also significant. Change portends. All will be transformed utterly but at the moment things seem not to change at all. In Pirandello, by contrast, there is a sense of no one knowing exactly where they are to begin with, of never having had those sureties of time and place and identity out of which Ibsen and Chekhov would construct at the very least the first act of their major works. Tragicomedy in its post-Chekhovian phase, in its modernist idiom, is a challenge to the domination of the rounded bourgeois personality, that literary heritage of the Enlightenment preserved into the twentieth century and the new age of Western liberalism. Naturally, its challenge echoes challenges in history to the security of the individual which have been more fundamental, the cyclical crises of corporate capitalism, the cataclysms of war, revolution and dictatorship. But as opposed to Brecht's more analytic and fabulist dissection of such things, it uses epistemological shock tactics in mounting a challenge to the centrality of the modern self.

The challenge to personality comes from the diminishing of character, but never its liquidation. If Expressionism claimed to liberate itself from the social constraints of naturalist plot by affirming the epic 'I',[2] tragicomedy seems to have done the opposite. It has robbed dramatic realism of that individuality which must oppose social constraint, which makes the moral dilemma of the trapped hero the central focus of dramatic action. It thus shares with the epic theatre of Brecht the wish to move away from the foregrounding of the individual, but does so by very different means from that of the gestus and the alienation-effect. It does not assume there is an objective reality which can be finally judged, which can first be dramatically constructed – instead of naturally represented – so that an audience can deliver a specific kind of verdict. Instead there is no vantage point from which any kind of special judgement can be made. Author, characters and audience share in a triangulated uncertainty which brings forth its own dramatic tensions. In order for this to happen, characters need to remain characters. They can never be reduced to ciphers of authorial manipulation or wider social forces. They are never convenient or reductive exemplars of anything. They remain human, all too human. As Ruby Cohn reminds us *à propos* of Beckett, his characters are never symbols, fictions or objects but always 'my people'.[3]

Tragicomedy forces us to question the certainty of self at the same time as it forces us in general to question the certainty of knowledge. The ideal of self-knowledge had grown out of the rational ideal of the scientific certainties of other forms of knowledge. Self-knowledge, it was assumed, could model itself on science and learn from its discoveries. But many forms of scientific enquiry in our century have shown us how little we know, and how each new discovery can expand the gaps that remain, while the new discoveries in weapons technology have led to the potential destruction of the planet. Science, as Oppenheimer reminds us in his description of the hydrogen bomb, is 'technically sweet', but also genocidal. The advance of global technologies in all spheres of life diminishes, as Weber and the critical theorists have warned, traditional ideals of individuality. Weber's rationalisation, Heidegger's *Das Man*, Marcuse's one-dimensional society and Adorno's 'administered world' are all prophetic warning concepts of the demise of the rational person, and of the commodified integration of the individual into a corporate and featureless world. Significantly the various scenarios for nuclear war invented by defence experts depend on elaborate game-playing with sophisticated computers, on endless hypothetical performances of apocalypse. They have their own 'endgame'. Death itself becomes a game.

Beckett and tragicomedy, however, cannot be taken purely as artistic exemplars of this imminent apocalypse which has been blended by the critical theorists out of war, technology, bureaucracy and corporate capitalism. The tragicomic emphasis on play suggests in addition a vital inner space which is more than just aesthetic. It is akin to Adorno's negative praxis, working against the system in its emphasis on a human playfulness which goes beyond scientific game-playing, which can be seen instead as a modernist transformation of Schiller's classic aesthetic. Paradoxically, modern consumerism lends itself to the enhancement of play, to its establishment as an axis of interior resistance to commodification. As art, tragicomedy is part of that resistance. It is authentic in Heidegger's sense, reflexive in Adorno's sense, and two-dimensional in Marcuse's grand though problematic scheme of human affairs. It has not been absorbed by electronic culture, nor is it a nostalgic tribute to a bygone age. The juxtaposition of play and commodification which is central to the tragicomic vision of the modern world suggests contradiction not elision, a tense co-existence of opposites not the elimination of the individual subject. On the other hand the dark helplessness of tragicomic characters challenges the facile conceptions of 'post-modernism', of its deliberate embrace of the commodity process, of the fun of pastiche and of the delight seen to exist in the limitless horizons of consumer promiscuity. Moreover, tragicomedy can never be reduced to an unwitting apology for modernist kitsch.

For tragicomedy is also a theatre of shock. If Beckett is as reflexive as Proust he can also be as stark and as shocking as Kafka. The tragicomic obliterates the historical distinction Adorno made between the aesthetic self-regard of High Modernism which had protected the artistic object from the invasion of a commodified documentary world and the dissonant world of *Metamorphosis* where the contemplative world of artistic appreciation is viscerally shattered by stark and inexplicable horror.[4] Lacking the violent immediacy of Artaud, tragicomedy still shows the continuity and unity of these separate modernist forms. If it is reflexive in its use of play and performance as human 'theatricality', it is equally stark in its use of shock effects which resist rational psychology or sociological continuity, which defy life-as-usual in order to provoke us into questioning our concept of the normal. It shows the horrors and suffering of contemporary humanity. But that humanity is not passive, and part of the modernist outrage is to show us that such horror cannot abolish laughter. The comic dreams and aspirations of those so hopelessly stunted they stand little chance of achieving anything are still signs of active hope. The gap between aspiration and deed, the bedrock of modern humour, is at its strongest as tragicomedy shows us in a world of victims. Its heroes are at times pathetic creatures, but through aspirations which will not die they still achieve a genuine pathos we cannot take away from them.

The reflexive use of play in tragicomedy parallels and prophesies the performative culture of Western consumer societies. But it also points out a central feature of consumer culture ignored by its most recent proclaimers. The claims variously made by Barthes, Lyotard, Deleuze and Baudrillard for a heterogeneous and decentred hedonistic world of post-modern consumption overlook the forms of self-dramatisation which are endemic in a consumer culture. To consume is also to perform. If cultural signs are seen purely as commodified myths that are mechanically generated, then not only is the process of producing them undervalued but so also is the impetus to create or re-produce them which they generate in their consumers. This impetus hinges more and more on performance. In the age of film and video, advertising dramatises its product more and more as a narrative spectacle which creates in its audience a mirror-image function of the desire to advertise. One responds to the advertising of a desired object not merely through the impulse to gratify, that is, through buying the object in order to consume it. One also responds to the ubiquity of advertising by using the product to advertise oneself.

Haug has suggested that in consumer culture commodities are aestheticised for profit, inducing the promise of gratification for needs which are often invented. The shop or boutique becomes a stage for the salesperson who displays goods like a performer.[5] But it would probably be truer to say that in the contemporary boutique, it is the buyer not the seller who is tempted by the myths of performance. The seller sells by encouraging the buyer to perform. To test-drive a fast new car is a rehearsal for high performance on a motorway, to try on expensive new clothing is a rehearsal for wearing it in a club or on the street, for a new kind of possible self-display. To consume here means not merely to gratify but also to imitate. Consumers mimic the style which attaches to the signs of their desired object. What excites desire is not merely the object but the dramatised performance associated with it on billboards, in magazines, TV commercials and department stores. Part of the attraction of consuming the object is to dramatise oneself in the act of consumption. The consumer object, whether it be a car, a form of perfume, a hi-fi, a pair of blue jeans or sneakers with the right label, is a necessary prop in the endless masquerade of self-performance. It is primarily the act of performing, not consuming, which devours and subjugates content. To consume nowadays contains not so much the *promesse de bonheur* but the promise of performing. The myth-making of desirable objects is inseparable from the competition between brands of objects to project that myth. In terms of their own mythology advertisers compete with other advertised objects of 'enhanced' performance by promising the enhancing of performance among those who consume them.

The paradox here is that tragicomedy seems not at all concerned with prosperity, conspicuous consumption or designer perform-ance. It is by comparison, a 'poor theatre' with minimal props and little surplus. But its outcast characters resemble at times latter-day consumers stripped of their adornments and their illusions, literal-ly unrecognisable, forced to act out their parts with no good reason for doing so. There is a provisional bracketing of the paraphernalia that are most desired in the world of consumption. Instead tragicomic characters perform with no cues or prompting and with no apparent motive. Bracketed out of the natural world, perform-ance has no cushion of meaning, no safety net. It is a severely bleak version of play as fate. Environment is no longer clear, tangible or rationally accessible. It is replaced by an inscrutable fate in which intention seems severed from human action, in which causality has been replaced by the randomness of chance. Yet without being environmental in the naturalist sense, or supernatural in the religious sense, fate still is an external force, the external something that determines human action but has no public face, no visible emanation. No longer in the lap of the gods, it is dispersed amidst the being of a profane world. It is a random encounter with those unseen accretions of culture which seem, to all the players in the game, tantalisingly just out of reach. Such accretions belong to the past, to myth, to wealth, to unseen forms of power. They are everywhere but here, never tangible or determinate. In this way, the game as fate becomes a mixture of chance and necessity whose respective ratios can never be fixed. The ultimate cause of anything can never be established. In the age of reason, the sense of human mastery is lost.

This leads us back to our central proposition. The play of tragicomedy is a haunting echo of our performative culture. The diminished Other of tragicomedy is the fractured double of the modern consumer. Of course, the stage is never a mirror. What its audience sees here is the shifting movement of depleted personas which are vaguely familiar but stripped bare of the artefacts of cultural identity, bleakly unadorned. This is not so much a world without objects but a world where most objects are deprived of cultural meaning and reduced inadvertently to junk. If the critical theorists mistakenly think it possible to consume without performing, tragicomedy shows us performing without consuming. We do not recognise ourselves in this (dis)guise. There is no place here for empathy. Our hearts do not go out to the cultural (de)relicts of our own civilisation. The footlights are a border, a necessary demarcation of different territories to be respected. For the characters of tragicomedy are 'strange' people performing in 'strange' ways and playing unfamiliar games. They are never us, never our-selves.

Whatever we see in these strange personas we do not recognise as something inhering in ourselves. On the other hand these strange personas we see on stage appear half the time not to recognise each other, or their own surroundings. Our own bewilderment is refracted by theirs, but therein lies the paradox. Their abject failure to recognise each other and the objects around them, their constant disremembering, is precisely what makes them strange. For that reason our failure to see anything normal in them is what makes us normal. Tragicomedy forces us back, uneasily, onto our fragile normality. We lose sight of our own doubles, of those traces of resemblance buried beneath the play of the culturally impoverished. And there is always the rightful temptation to laughter. Laughter, after all, will distance us from the bewildering objects of our gaze and the reversals of fortune they do not understand, which seem to go round in circles and lead nowhere. But the laughter here is not really a laughing away of human folly, because it is shadowed by the darkness of human downfall which cannot be exhausted by rational explanation. We laugh at the folly of their failure to recognise their fate and yet that fate does not go away. We, the audience, are left with its residue.

As opposed to Brecht's 'complex seeing', tragicomedy gives us double vision. We fail to recognise the figures of our diminished doubles who in turn fail to recognise each other. Our failure, we imagine, is healthy. Theirs is absurd. In the act of distancing ourselves from our fleeting shadows we grow closer towards them. For that very act of disassociation confirms a repressed likeness. It is a likeness based on helplessness. If we were as helpless, and hopeless, as they in the world in which *we* live, we would not survive. But in a world of potential mass destruction everyone is ultimately helpless. If we bury that helplessness because it threatens the sense we have of our own individuality, tragicomedy buries the apocalypse which runs through its pages. It is a drama for an age of controlled apocalypse. But it is so obliquely, a modernist commentary dramatised for the occasion of our epoch. It is a set of chamber pieces in an electronic culture which measures its spectacles in terms of size and glitter and noise. The texts of Beckett, Pinter and Shepard are precise gems, jewelled miniatures amidst this vast and endless explosion of instant culture. They may look frail, but like the beaten gold of which Yeats speaks in 'Byzantium', they are magnificent and irreducible. They tell us, more than other writing in the second half of this century, why we have lived through an age of tragicomedy. They show us why we laugh amidst darkness and feel sorrow and despair in the midst of elation. Their 'play' pulses through the depths of our uncertain and fragmentary living. It thumbs its nose at the gods but equally at the jargon of human Reason. It is as much as anyone could dare ask.

2
Play and Performative Culture

In the theatre, identity is a construct of performance, the stage an arena of illusion. Often the word 'persona' seems more precise than the word 'character' with its echoes of the complete and observed 'person'. Indeed if we continue to call players characters it is precisely because we have fallen prey to their vibrant powers of illusion. They embody the passing illusion of a self-contained life. For all characters are actors who perform, who don metaphorical masks, whose job is usually to realise the persona of someone else's invention. The emerging identity of that persona is a balancing act between the actor's self, the character that is performed and what might be accepted by the audience as reality in the world beyond the stage. Such a world is always important. The arena of illusion must make reference to a Beyond that is both more real and yet more remote. Once it comes into performance, this world of the Beyond is also trapped by performance, enslaved and wrenched out of its proper habitus. In capturing the Otherness of the world beyond, performance expresses its own nature simultaneously with that part of the world it has briefly captured. The force of dramatic impact upon the spectator usually leads to one conclusion. It is the performance not the world which at that moment is the more real.

Here there must always be conventions of performance to sustain the illusion. These are largely rhetorical, convincing us of the action we see through socially pertinent gestures.[1] But in any drama which endures, such conventions have, at first, to be fought for and won. If they are not, they go quickly stale. Each new dramatic form struggles to find a true rhetoric and this can be anything but conventional. The century-old 'scandals' of *A Doll's House* or *Miss Julie* have lately been matched by the 'scandals' of *Waiting for Godot*, *Saved*, and *The Romans in Britain*. If convention becomes complacency, then in the end it must be dismantled. The theatre must constantly surprise us. At times it must shock us too.

10

The thrust of modernism in our own century goes even further. It quickens this process of struggle and change. It suggests that performance should *never* be conventional. It must surprise, dislocate, fragment and disorient, forcing the spectator to uncomfortable judgement. No convention can ever be taken for granted in such bold un-conventions of performance.

A century ago the case was somewhat different. Despite the controversies they caused in their own lifetimes, Ibsen and Chekhov forged a dramatic realism which suggested the closure and coherence of fictional narrative. Indeed Bakhtin has referred in passing to the essential 'novelness' of the late nineteenth-century theatre.[2] Like Strindberg, Hauptmann and the French Naturalists, Ibsen and Chekhov had extended realist ontology into the theatre, creating recognisable illusions of space and time, a highly 'natural' world within the confines of the proscenium arch. All used the stage as a metonymic resource for showing lifelike objects, for making accurate reductions of social scale even when, as in the Abbey production of *Riders to the Sea*, retaining exact measurements of fishermen's cottages. The stage, moreover, was turned into precise three-walled rooms with chairs, sofas, bookcases, pianos and duelling pistols.[3] While the audience watched, voyeuristically, through the open fourth wall, the objects of nature and culture alike were endowed with key symbolic values. *The Wild Duck* and *The Seagull* may now seem like natural titles for naturalist plays, but only because they once, like General Gabler's pistols, had to be naturalised as objects with a new and forbidding value. If the stage play could not match the novel's historical power, its open narrative was countered in Ibsen by the compressed eruptions of the past into the present and in Chekhov by powerful reduced forms of the collective in which the group becomes a microcosm of the wider society.

Other vital uses of dramatic space gave Ibsen and Chekhov a tragic dimension which made much of the naturalism which followed seem dull by comparison. In most of their work there is a constant, oblique play on cultural periphery which finds its later echo in Synge and Lorca, an ironic gloss on historical 'backwardness' in a rapidly industrialising Europe.[4] Evocations of fiord and steppe, the wild Atlantic and the oven heat of Andalucia as realities just beyond the gaze, a wildness of nature much too great to be naturalised by a naturalistic stage, take tragedy out of the bourgeois domain. But as Europe continued to modernise, the sense of cultural periphery changed and modernisms found nurture not on the margin but at the centre. Franco Moretti has suggested that Germany is at the centre of the battlefield for modernity.[5] The German city became the key to the avant-garde and to modernism. Its theatre was rivalled by its Expressionist painting and poetry and its new metropolitan fiction. Elsewhere in Europe it was challenged by the imagistic poem and the self-conscious narrative, by the epiphany and the interior monologue. How could the play hope to dramatise the inward turn of Proust and Mann, Joyce and Woolf? How could it ever 'stage' preconscious language? The crisis found its strongest answer, following Strindberg, in the 'station dramas' of Expressionism and then in Pirandello's theatre of illusion. Expressionism was at the core of the new impetus in painting, poetry, the cinema and the theatre. In drama, its freeing of the subject from the trap of immediate circumstance produced the paradox of a depersonalised subjectivity. The expressionist heroes of Georg Kaiser became the ciphers of transindividual structures of feeling in which public role was more important than private name. Williams's claim that the movement extended naturalist premises rather than breaking with them is only half true.[6] For if their heroes escaped the clutter of domestic circumstance to become the vehicles of cosmic feeling, then they were no longer distinctive or unique as bourgeois personalities. The break with Ibsen or Chekhov was almost complete. Only O'Neill's early plays successfully forged an ingenious match of Expressionist and naturalist forms. The ship's stokehole of *The Hairy Ape*, the hallucinated fears of the doomed black hero in *The Emperor Jones* and the shrinking walls of *All God's Chillun' Got Wings* visually projected the traumas of highly individualised American heroes. The psychic conflicts of Ibsen and Strindberg were still maintained. Yet even O'Neill sensed that a drama of social relationships had to go beyond the Expressionist versions of the epic 'I'. To his mind, a new Freudian dramaturgy of the Self and the Other was required.

It was the formidable challenge of Freud and Joyce to which O'Neill responded in his ambitious play of interior monologue, *Strange Interlude*. The play was a test case for the new limitations exposed by fiction and psychoanalysis.[7] O'Neill used a form of dramatic aside which went beyond soliloquy or confidential statements of intent to the audience. The long monologues by Nina Leeds and her 'three men' are confessional statements erupting into the middle of dialogue, during which the other characters have to freeze themselves out of the posture of listening. Such intimate thoughtspeech is intended as a gloss on the secrets of the pre-conscious, a conscious demystifying by which O'Neill tries to obliterate the ambiguities of pause, silence and double meaning that are Ibsen's legacy. The play fails magnificently. It leads not into the darker recesses of the psyche but into the obvious rationalisations and hypocrises of bourgeois morality. It thus works as superb comic melodrama where O'Neill had wished instead for a tragic dimension. Since the dramatic suspense plays on what might be confessed but never is, the play's breath-taking leaps in time turn it into serial melodrama. The Ibsenist subtext, which profoundly inspired Freud, is replaced by a drama which leaves us with no obvious secrets, no stone left unturned. Certainly it lays bare the mechanisms of social order, the way in which American families of a certain period might suppress knowledge of transgressions which are their potential undoing. But this hardly goes to the depths of the human soul. O'Neill's asides have the composure of a finished language which, as Joyce and Eliot have shown, the pre-conscious levels of the mind could never possess.

O'Neill thus fails to dramatise the logic of association or the imagistic fragment for which subtext and silence are more plausible risks. Even if we accept the convention of 'thoughtspeech', we must still ask how much of it is truthful, and how much 'performance'? Here performance is a double-edged sword. O'Neill, more than any other playwright, raises the question of *the performance of authenticity*. The composed language of the articulate voice, even in the throes of confession, still suggests a kind of performance, a performance inseparable from the elaborate rationalisation of what the speaker intends doing or has already done. Only in his masterpiece *Long Day's Journey into Night* does O'Neill come close to mastering the rationalisations of confessional speech. Here he converts thoughtspeech into riveting dialogue, into speaking *and* listening. Among the Tyrones, confession is mutual, the whole family sharing its claustrophobia, each bewildered in turn by the vertigo of the confession, exhausted, challenged and unmasked, where the unmasker in turn is destined to be exposed. O'Neill's quadrangulated vertigo constantly undercuts the 'truth' of confession and countertruths themselves turn into vulnerable confessions as the play spirals into an infinite regress of performance and counterperformance.

While O'Neill is one of the prime beneficiaries of Stanislavskian realism, his roots are still strongly in an earlier American melodrama. His melodramatic suspense often works as a counterpoint to the 'presencing' of the Stanislavkian persona, particularly in the figure of Mary Tyrone. Mary starts out as the domestic centre of the play, its matriarchal presence, but ends up as a decentred persona, a solitary woman in an opium trance who recognises nothing and nobody, who reminisces about James as if he were not there. Home has long since been a vacuum and life now is wishing that life as lived had never been lived at all. The wife-mother ends up as 'Ophelia', the wraith, the ghost on whose possible entrance the audience and the male Tyrones hang in suspense. Her tangible absence, her uncanny 'lurking' at the back of stage, blends with the opium trance which blinds her to knowledge of herself and her family. O'Neill returns us to tragic convention by forcing the male Tyrones to recognise the full nature of their collective tragedy, but only by seeing that Mary lacks any kind of recognition at all.

In other ways worlds apart, the tragicomic outsiders of Jean Genet and Samuel Beckett are closer to the 'absent' Mary Tyrone than to O'Neill's earlier proletarians of substance. This, historically, is what defines the origins of modern tragicomedy. While Brecht's epic theatre sublated his non-bourgeois subjects into gestic carriers of Judgement and History, Genet and Beckett embedded theirs in structures of play and performance. As an emergent tragicomic form *Waiting for Godot* thrusts performance-as-convention into the realm of existential play. What is left of 'truth' spirals into confusion and endless relativity as the known worlds of self, motive, personality disappear. In Genet, Stanislavsky's insistence on psychic presence gives way to the tempting perils of vertiginous role-playing. As the tragic gives way to the tragicomic, a new theatre of play is created, a *ludic* theatre of shock and dislocation.

To speak of ludic theatre and not a 'theatre of the absurd' is to make a vital shift of emphasis. Playwrights as diverse as Pinter, Bond, Stoppard, Orton, Soyinka, Fugard, Albee, Kopit, Shepard and Mamet have inherited its legacy. The boundaries of definition need to be redrawn. While Mary Tyrone's disappearing act is crucial to understanding the contemporary theatre it is still a world away from *Godot* and *The Maids*. More importantly, we need to place ludic theatre in the divided history of modernism, as part indeed of that second wave of modernism Frank Kermode has called neo-modernism, distinguishing it from the High Modernism of 1910–1925 in which Expressionism played such an important part.[8] Not only was it a renaissance but also a response to the earlier crisis in dramatic form which High Modernism had provoked, a challenging answer which middle-period O'Neill failed to give. It is thus an aesthetic alternative to the early modernist novel, to the deeper psychic absences of *Ulysses* with their interior estrangement of a Jewish Irishman adrift on Dublin streets, to the uncanny absence of the dead Mrs Ramsey which haunts the later sections of *To the Lighthouse*, to the agonising absence of Caddy in *The Sound and the Fury* who becomes 'present' only in the rather different demented memories of her three brothers. The ludic theatre echoes these lyric dissolutions of stable identity but by different means, through the enlargement of what Adorno has called the aesthetic of shock. In all twentieth-century art he sees shock at the heart of the new 'terror' of modernism.[9] After Kafka, we might add Genet and Beckett.

Modernism, however, also comprises, as Octavio Paz has stressed, an aesthetics of rupture.[10] Here tragicomedy becomes unthinkable without the work of Luigi Pirandello. Pirandello breaks more decisively with pre-modernist drama than the Expressionists. In his plays rupture entails a decisive break between role and persona, and between truth and illusion. The two breaks are indissolubly linked. Absolute claims about truth and illusion are impossible where the ontological status of characters can never be fully established. To live in a world in which Einsteinian relativity has destroyed objective space and time is to live in a world where persons can create their own fantasies and promote them as real. 'Henry the Fourth' in *Henry the Fourth* continues throughout his life to play the part he was playing in a pageant when he fell from his horse but at a certain point he becomes conscious of his masquerade. If he pretends to be mad, he also pretends to be sane, finally confessing the awareness of the mask he has been wearing. The rupture of role and persona, exploited so brilliantly by Pirandello, adds a comic frame through which the tragic predicament of 'Henry the Fourth' is filtered. The comedy is no light relief, no porter's scene in *Macbeth*, no calm before the storm. It is the indispensable framework for the tragedy of dissolved identity, the tragedy of the diminished hero who no longer knows who he is, who lives out his life, at times consciously, in a masquerade.

The comic framework of tragic enactment is even more pronounced in *Six Characters in Search of an Author*. The stunning role-reversal, where a cynical group of actors become a captive audience subjected to an impromptu family drama almost too raw and painful to be staged, is a brilliant gloss on the nature of theatricality. The amateur 'drama' dismissed by the actors as untheatrical is then made compelling by the playwright. Pirandello trades on our sense of tragedy and suffering as states too primal to be dramatised by those who have not undergone the same emotions. But in fact *he* has dramatised them, exposing theatrical artifice by creating it in its most subtle guise. It is an intricate play on the performance of authenticity light years away from O'Neill's dogged loyalty to the Ibsenist illusion of reality. The producer and the actors tell the family their story is untheatrical and cannot be performed since it ignores the question of dramatic impact upon its audience. Later when the producer agrees to perform it, members of the family claim the professional acting travesties their own feelings and obscures the truth. The chasm of relativity which yawns is far greater than in O'Neill where the ontological status of the characters is firmly established. Here the characters have not found their true 'author' to give them dramatic life, while the actors find they have no reality outside their profession, which is largely to produce illusions

Pirandello thus sets the trap of an infinite regress from which his decentred characters cannot escape. In the culture of the twentieth century there has been a growing uncertainty over the nature of self and its relationship to others. In his drama that is transferred into a divide between role and person which the stage persona cannot bridge. The various masquerades induced by this hiatus bring welcome comic relief. But the failure to bridge the gap brings tragic suffering in its wake. Pirandello's fusion of the comic and the tragic differs from that of Chekhov which works on a single continuum, on the variations in mood and circumstance of definitive characters with a dramatic solidity. The perturbed father of *Six Characters* accuses the actors who recreate his family on-stage of merely playing games. In his eyes, the actors create an illusion which cruelly mimics reality. Meanwhile the family feels itself doomed never to find the exact means of performing its real-life tragedy, until tragedy unexpectedly strikes. Pirandello prefigures the role-reversals of Genet and Shepard where the dividing of roles is less absolute. Where Pirandello dissolves selfhood into uncertainty, the Other in Genet provides a safety net, an object which the decentred subject can aspire to become. But this tangible goal is itself an illusion. The coveted Other is just as elusive as the dissolving self. It is only the *image* of the Other's self which can be appropriated. The desire for the Other is thus utopian, and merely masks self-negation. The rupture remains.

In the aesthetic history of shock, tragicomedy extends the earlier patterns of dissonance and subversion in Schoenberg, Picasso and Kafka. For Adorno, the latter are the chief exemplars of an art which defies the commodifications of administered culture. But the dramaturgy of shock is something about which he is never specific. Reduced by other critics to the fetishistic concept of 'the absurd', it is then vulgarised into a notion of all human experience as absurd. Our starting-point must surely lie in the new structures of feeling which Pirandello made possible through his unique fusion of rupture and shock, where the self appears to the audience as an image in a shattered mirror. It is this fusion which is developed in Genet's role-reversals where the illusory embrace of otherness creates new forms of self-negation, and in Beckett's vacant landscapes where human play confronts a universal void. The dominant structures of feeling here stress two kinds of experience, playfulness and the breakdown of perception. These we can call *play* and *disrecognition*.

Disrecognitions are forms of forgetting, failures or refusals to recognise the objects of one's surroundings. We can see them as a modernist shattering of forms of perceptual recognition. Bergson had suggested two basic forms of recognition, *habitual* and *attentive* recognition.[10] The first involves a sensory–motor reaction to a familiar object but the second involves a more selective and abstract description of the thing recognised which depends, to a large extent, on recollection. Forms of disrecognising in tragicomedy seem to move in the opposite direction. Failures of recollection initially destroy the powers of attentive recognition and then proceed to damage the habitual recognition of familiar objects. This is in no sense a rational dismantling of ordinary perception. On the contrary it entails the use of dramatic shocks to dismember ordinary seeing and create new structures of feeling. Disrecognitions are both shock-effects and ways of seeing, historic equivalents of the metonymic symbols of Ibsen and Chekhov, the claustrophobic estrangements of O'Neill, the V-effects of Brecht. In their classic form, in *Godot* and *Endgame*, comedies of error are mixed with deeper tragic refusals of non-recognition. Together they threaten the identities of Self and Other. Both point to damaged powers of perception on the part of their hapless characters. Loss of memory, confusions of time and place, failure to recognise others or name names are commonplace. Often there is a deeper and more wilful existential refusal to recognise, a disremembering which borders on bad faith. In the drama which follows Beckett, such shocking un-convention becomes a dramatic convention. After initial confusion or outrage, audiences become prepared for the breakdowns of recognition. But even if they expect its general use, they still remain thrown by precise examples. The brevity of the two-act play is a short, sharp shock which disconcerts the emotions more than it purges them. For that reason tragicomedy remains a thorn in the flesh of convention, a challenge to naturalistic complacencies. Disrecognitions continually disturb. Not only do they break particular codes. They challenge the fixity of codes as such.

The role of play is equally vital. The work of Genet and Pinter maintains the modernist 'outrage' of a labile sexuality, but it also subsumes that sexuality under the outrage of a playfulness about themes considered serious. Whether sexuality explodes out of the elaborate illusions of *The Balcony*, or the taut, shocking obscenities of *The Homecoming*, it is still defined by the play of illusion or the play of obscenity. Play is tragicomedy's elusive response to the moral void it perceives in modern culture. It can be dramatised as boredom and invention, simulation and performance, extemporising and make-believe, as anything to ward off, however briefly, the loss of human control. It is much more than a set of clever language games, and Caillois's ingenious typology of games, in which civilisation progresses from games of mimicry and vertigo to games of chance and competition, hardly seems to apply here at all.[11] In tragicomedy, no kind of game is excluded. Everything is fair game.

All play, including the play-within-the-play, is a vital part of theatrical tradition. But in tragicomedy game-playing is more pervasive, shadowed even in its most amusing forms by the ubiquity of terror. The failures of game-playing can be amusing, but the game itself usually terrifies. It shows the comic fallibility of mortals at the edge of an abyss. Endlessly reflexive play and the rapid improvisations of game-playing lead to bewilderment rather than certainty. There appear to be no rules and play in the modern theatre lacks the fixity of a discrete form. It contradicts those classic elements of play which Huizinga in *Homo Ludens* found to be fundamental to Western societies. For him the essence of play lay in its lack of seriousness and the bounded nature of its rituals.[12] Typically the rite is secluded or inclusive, cutting itself off from the banal, serious and profane aspects of daily life. Play creates its own ritual spaces, setting it apart from the monotony of the familiar and the tedium of obligation. But ludic theatre dissolves this duality, and makes it impossible to draw the boundary between what is play and what is serious, what is performance and what is profane. For Beckett, the game is desperate and serious: for his successors no less so. The power to ad-lib, however comic, is the key to survival. The tragicomic illustrates a neglected truth which Ehrmann has succinctly noted. If we seek to define play, in the same breath we seek to define reality and to define culture.[13] In the nature of its play, the tragicomic exposes one of the key cultural realities of modernity, the constant stress on human performance.

Before we uncover this complex relationship, we have to say what ludism is not. It is not the formalised spectacles of Peter Schaffer which exaggerate symbol and rite, using them as cannon fodder for the reified battles of Reason and the Irrational. The existential game cannot be prised apart to offer up such a facile dualism. The lesson of Beckett is clear. In the absence of any transcending value, where God is invisible, where it seems impossible to ascribe a meaning to being, play is deritualised and demythologised. In *Godot* it appears, deceptively, to have no history or place of its own. It is a response to disrecognition, to the lack of known landmarks and familiar names. Yet in Beckett, Pinter and Shepard the play we encounter does have its own cultural referents in a particular time, a particular place, a particular world. Two plays which strongly bear the imprint of Beckett illustrate this self-contextualising of play in tragicomedy.

In Athol Fugard's *The Island*, two black prisoners on Robbens Island, victims of apartheid, argue about and then rehearse their *ad hoc* version of the trial of Antigone with which they hope to placate their white captors. Like Hamlet's 'Slaying of Gonzago' the performance of the play has its ulterior motive. But it is more. The play's 'rehearsal' is rent through with those Beckettian features of the everyday which translate so well into the fact of imprisonment. There is a constant play on waiting for release. The theme of Antigone's punishment by Creon for burying Polynices is an apt symbol of their own punishment by the Pretoria regime. The endless arguments about who shall play Creon and who Antigone echo the play-ful role-reversals of Genet which are amusing but deadly serious. Thus the two convicts play at the conception of their play, sometimes comically, sometimes with pathos, as if playing competitively in a game of chance whose outcome they cannot know. In Sam Shepard's *The Tooth of Crime*, a play about the rock culture of the late sixties, the showdown between the competing stars is part boxing match, part street-car race, part Western gunfight, part DJ rapping contest. The game is deadly serious, a matter of life and death. But it is scarcely lifelike. It is a mythic hybrid ritual embracing so many things all at once in the junk culture from which it is lifted that its compression into a single encounter seems nothing less than a dramatic miracle. It is theatrically compelling because it is a game of fragments, a ritual without a code. The showdown works because it seems to contain all of American culture yet cannot be pinned down. It finally eludes definition.

From Beckett we also know that play accelerates the passing of time. Didi and Gogo make up games to assuage the boredom of waiting for Godot, encouraging Pozzo and Lucky to 'perform' in turn for them. George and Martha, cheery campus hosts of *Who's Afraid of Virginia Woolf?*, invent malicious party games such as 'Humping the Hostess' and 'Getting the Guests' to abase themselves in front of their naive young visitors who they then humiliate. In Edward Bond's *Saved* the killing of Pam's baby starts off as a lark with a pram in the park, a recognisable way that Cockney lads create of 'having a laugh'. But it ends barbarically with the stoning of the defenceless child. At times the characters of the tragicomic seem to be staging their own psychodramas, a multitude of 'plays' which reflexively gloss the playwright's invention of the play in which they are taking part. On the surface this might appear to parallel the device of authorial signature in what is called 'post-modernist' fiction. But it is rather different. The deadly seriousness of the game, its existential desperation and power to shock make it a party to modernist terror. Not only are the temptations of a blank 'post-modern' pastiche refused.[14] They are also meaningless. However bewildering, the game is still fate. The play of the ludic character is too serious to be the play of the manipulative author.

Further contrast between drama and fiction can be seen in the contrasting use of names. In the fiction of Gaddis, Pynchon and

Vonnegut we find exotic and allegorical forms of naming, an extravagant yet satirical fullness. Ludism by contrast deals mainly in single names or even, as in *Endgame*, single names of single syllables. Use of either Christian names *or* surnames, seldom both together, suggests a fragile identity, the living of a purgatorial existence where names are no guarantee of recognition. In Shepard's *La Turista*, Kent and Salem are named after popular cigarette brands. In *Curse of the Starving Class*, the paired names of mother and daughter, Emma and Ella, and father and son, Weston and Wesley, sound like generational variants of the same person. In Beckett's most famous play, the most named and significant person, Godot, never appears while Vladimir and Estragon call each other by different names than the ones their playwright has given them. While so many characters are called by single names, by mistaken names and by more than one name, then naming can no longer stand as a mark of fixed identity. Often it appears the opposite, the mark of an absence of identity, the reduction of the fullness of naming to a sound signifying almost nothing.

False naming and forgetting are symbolic denials of a symbolic world. Yet these denials occur most often in the sub-worlds of the socially excluded. The catharses of classical and Renaissance tragedy are as impossible here as the modern empathies of Ibsen and O'Neill. In comparing *Godot* with *Oedipus Rex* and *Hamlet*, Bruce Wilshire has shown how Beckett's plays break down with uncanny coherence the basic forms of tragic empathy.[15] Both Oedipus and Hamlet are tragic heroes with whom audiences identify because they are noble beings displaced to the realm of the problematic from the realm of natural authority and self-control. Audiences become directly involved in the combatant's tragic struggle against an insuperable problem which eventually destroys him. Both Oedipus (unconsciously) and Hamlet (consciously) extend the remit of their natural authority by replacing their fathers and are duly punished. But there is no way that Beckett's downtrodden anti-heroes can replace or 'stand in' for Godot. They are, Wilshire states, 'as frail and insubstantial as wraiths'.[16] Beckett also breaks with naturalist conventions of human control. In *Hedda Gabler* the fate of the absent Eilert Loevberg who dies off-stage in a brothel is given dramatic presence by Hedda's fanatical but unsuccessful attempts to direct that fate, as if by remote control. But Didi and Gogo have no firmer a conception of the absent Godot at the end than they do at the beginning. The only relationship they have with him is that of waiting. Nothing that is not local, immediate, present at hand, *on-stage*, can finally exist. The role-reversals in *The Maids* can be seen in a similar light. Claire stands in for Madame and Solange for Claire but both quickly revert to type when she returns. Impersonation of her authority turns out to be an illusion, usurpation of her role the erotic fantasy of the subjugated.

Shock tactics enhance the tragicomic pathos of the exploited and the derelict. Beckett's vagrants, Genet's deviant underlings, Fugard's black servants and prisoners, Shepard's marginal families, even Soyinka's drivers and specialists, all have one thing in common. They briefly thrive on the comic menace of play and disrecognising. At the same time they are its victims. The territorial jousts of Pinter's working-class Londoners can tempt the spectator amidst their menace to a tense, uneasy laughter. But all lack, in some degree, the kind of self-knowledge or insight which can bring hope to their future. In general, the realities of their psychic dereliction surface only now and again from the hilarious and terrifying performance of confusion. In Pinter self-knowledge is something to be evaded or repressed. But that constant repression takes its toll. The tactics of evasion and repression take over from their deeper reasons. Goals are supplanted by means. Existence becomes a matter of strategy. Moral issues are first avoided and finally go unrecognised. There are few clear recognitions of moral dilemma because, in the end, there is no clear field of vision. The tragicomic world is one in which the ideologies of a dominant culture are always opaque, but equally where a liberal conscience of ambiguous resistance to such ideology has no place. Its heroes do not judge on moral terms, for conscience is a luxury they do not possess.

The tragicomic challenge to conscience is one of the most powerful of modernism's challenges to the dominance in the Western world of a liberal ideology of individualism. It is, however, very different from Nietzsche's nihilistic prophecy of the death of man. Character is not eliminated, personality never liquidated. In tragicomedy characters continue to have individual identities. But its pathos derives very precisely from a gap between conscience and action which can never be bridged. Its characters continue to shock us because they lack any sign of those moral capacities which liberal philosophers have attributed to rational persons. Tragicomedy throws down the gauntlet. It challenges the complacency surrounding the Enlightenment ideals of rationality, citizenship and individual self-knowledge which have all been recycled in diluted form as part of the sensibility of liberal optimism in the West since the Second World War. Its emergence repeats the dissonant relationship between art and ideology to be found in High Modernism's earlier challenge to the jargon of Progress. It is a sharp, visionary response to the shortcomings of a rationalist world-view which tries to match the ideal citizen to an ideal future. For tragicomedy acknowledges neither the 'citizen' nor the future.

Moral failure and social dereliction are thus inseparable from the failures of selfhood and self-knowledge. The truth of the world is often evaded, but the truth of the self even more so. Albee's questioning title *Who's Afraid of Virginia Woolf?* makes a distinct challenge. It is a challenge to play games with the most intimate forms of modernism's psychic truths, going one stage further than O'Neill in transferring the performance of the authentic into the world of relativity. The authentic is played with, as well as performed, so that it is always in danger of losing any connection with reality. Albee's play moves dramatically towards a final revelation, but there is no revelation to be had, for revelation itself is absorbed into the endless repetitions of play. The desire to reveal the inner self is shown up even more radically as an illusion in the work of Genet. Watching *The Balcony* or *The Maids* one might naively suspect that Genet's sexual politics intend to uncover the inner truths of repressed desire, sexual truths that are both secret and substantial, the veritable libido of the 'real' self. But his 'truths' are not libidinal at all. They turn out to be impulses to abandon the self and take on instead the role of the coveted Other. They express the impulse to escape from selfhood and disperse it into nothingness. When Claire and Solange play at being Mistress and Maid they are challenging the authority they love and hate with a brittle vanity. Needless to say, the challenge quickly collapses. The socially anonymous clients of Irma's brothel in *The Balcony* play out the desired roles of Bishop, Judge, General and Chief of Police in a house of desire which is equally a house of illusion. If illusion cannot triumph without desire, then desire cannot triumph without illusion. Genet thus invokes desire as a complex illusion real in its consequences.

Tragicomedy still has a more conventional rival in the drama of bourgeois conscience, and has in no way superseded it. On the contrary it has learned to coexist with it. But such drama has been increasingly bedevilled by the uncertainty of its dramatic conventions, the abject failure, at times, to find substitutes for Stanislavskian certainty. *Altona, All That Fall, Sweet Bird of Youth, A Delicate Balance, Inadmissible Evidence, Equus* and *The Real Thing* have all in different ways been symptoms of the same crisis. All have lost the means of dramatising the key dilemmas of bourgeois conscience with any emotional power or intellectual clarity. Each step taken outside the naturalist frame of reference seems hasty, unplanned or capricious. But part of the problem lies in the current advantage which has been gained by other cultural forms. The post-war Anglo-American novel has produced a copious fiction of the domestic lives of the English and the American bourgeoisie. More important, the cinema from the late fifties onward has superseded the theatre in its complex explorations of bourgeois conscience. After Neo-realism, the films of Antonioni, Bergman, Bertolucci, Buñuel, Resnais, Rohmer and Visconti have together offered a more complex and powerful dissection of the European bourgeoisie than their rivals in the theatre. And they have done so through uncompromising innovation in modernist forms.

The modernist *auteurs* of the sixties, film directors, have become the true heirs to Ibsen, Strindberg and Chekhov.[17] That it happened then was partly because sound, colour, the wide lens and the mobile camera had been unavailable at the time of High Modernism. But equally it depended on the use of such technologies to create new forms, to create within the moving frame a unique fusion of painting, narrative and performance. It also depended on the viability of the prosperous middle classes in a new consumer society as a collective modernist subject. One also finds, looking at the best work of Antonioni, Pasolini, Bergman and Buñuel uncanny echoes of modern tragic drama, peripheral landscapes of Europe which in film have become landscapes of the mind, a 'peripheral vision' which the film-maker, through sheer stylistic power, uses to alienate the seeing eye. This form of alienation, typical of modern tragedy at its best, has been subsumed by film narrative. Even Pinter in his literary adaptations for film seems to have recognised that pure ludism cannot compete with the modernist landscape of mind. Instead approving audiences of dramatic realism or modernist film might see the figures of ludic drama as eccentric pathologies who very occasionally send them into a state of shock. Can they really be interested in such helpless eccentrics? Is the plight of the latter really universal? Do they tell us anything about modernity at all?

The riposte to this surely lies in our recent history. We do acknowledge the modernist challenge of tragicomedy to modernity. Tragicomic heroes strike a chord with us because they embody a fundamental paradox. They are willing players in a game they do not always control or understand, but are also astute inventors of their own moves and rituals, very much like the real-estate salesmen in David Mamet's *Glengary Glen Ross*. They play for high stakes in a game they cannot win, and which in a sense controls them. Both their lack of control and their play against impossible odds can distance us from them. They offend both our sense of selfhood and our sense of reason. Thematically, that offence is often naturalised by their abject social position, or by the fear of losing a position itself marginal, a recurrent theme in Pinter, Mamet and Shepard. This distancing effect intensifies the existing barriers to empathy. But it does something more. It enables tragicomedy to challenge those cultural conventions of 'natural' control so crucial to daily middle-class life, those complex forms of rational control over circumstance made possible by material success, specialised knowledge and cultural capital. It challenges the myth of rationality in the modern technological world. It cues us to the necessary but very flawed world of modern Reason, and we already know the pitfalls. We sense, as Freud and the critical theorists have asserted, that rationalities are in part psychic rationalisations, symbolic constructs of the quotidian made possible by the prospect of the material advantage they might bring. And we are clearly uneasy. The tragicomic plays, at times devastatingly, upon this unease.

Tragicomedy can hardly hope or wish to produce a rational critique of rationality. Nonetheless, its ludism challenges bourgeois myths of natural control by showing us circumstances in which they do not operate. Play and disrecognition are structures of feeling which contest much more than just rational enlightenment and self-knowledge. The neo-modernist renaissance of which tragicomedy has been a part is largely apocalyptic in tone.[18] In the midst of economic growth and prosperity in the West, defence

preparations for nuclear war have established a slavish dependence on game theory which makes its hypothetical 'plays' as
terrifying as anything drama could envisage. Complex weapons
systems appear to assume reified forms which can never be fully
dismantled, forms which Marcuse has suggested come to dominate the mentality of their controllers.[19] In the near future, with the
probable advent of the SDI, Star Wars will be simulated simultaneously in space and on the video screens of billion-dollar
computers. As the old-fashioned geographic 'theatre of war' is
made redundant by electronic screens and signals and space
trajectories, the future of the planet could be decided in a single
afternoon by the most expensive form of game-playing in history.[20]
Play here simply becomes unimaginable. The nuclear fear which
has generated anxiety and pessimism among successive younger
generations can hardly be expected to fade away.[21] If the playful
and the apocalyptic are connected in nuclear game-playing then
the techno-nuclear and consumerist dimensions of Western
societies are also connected as twin sources of economic prosperity. In a scenario that is totally surreal, pleasure stands next to
genocide.

Here tragicomedy, which is not surreal, lays bare something at
the core of our daily life which is usually suppressed, our sense of a
loss of control. Its sense of our cosmic helplessness makes the
individual breakdown of bourgeois conscience on the stage often
seem little more than a tortuous tantrum. That helplessness is
never central or total, but it is firmly residual, something which can
never be overcome. Loss of control is a form of *Dasein* in which
rational persons sporadically feel themselves at the mercy of an
external fate which seems to imitate supernatural fate but is an
accretion of human error and folly. That sense exists *in spite of* our
personal powers of existential inventiveness, and in spite of the
global privileges of the West. Tragicomedy appeals to us, at times
at a pre-conscious level, because it probes the disparity between a
greater sense of subjective freedom and a greater loss of objective
control. In a consumer age, cultural individualism can celebrate
shallow and transient victories, but only in the shadow of technologies which threaten extinction. Each new generation, as we
have seen, lives through a teenage fear of such extinction which
maintains its traces well into adult life. A fear which at one level
may well give rise to the gory effects of shock-horror movies has
led at a deeper level to the modernist decimation of a sure and

certain world and shown us there may be deeper reasons too for the performative impulse and its desperations.

Play in tragicomedy is indeed inseparable from the increasing role of performance in Western culture. Moreover, our idea of performance has taken on a new meaning since the theories of Erving Goffman. His astounding work has been a two-edged sword. Astoundingly prophetic of the new performative cultures of Western societies, it embodies still a nominalism which finally destroys its own insights. Goffman's dramaturgical metaphors have, from the start, a very myopic view of personality. The way in which people express themselves is part of their nature. Between the self and performance there are no clear boundaries. Goffman's division of a primary, opaque world of selfhood beneath the 'mask' and a secondary world of social selfhood which entails 'performance' and 'impression management' is at best tenuous and never absolute. Despite our doubts and uncertainties, how we express ourselves is part of what we are. Goffman's insight is to show that the fracturing of modern self entails performances which can contradict one another, which often induce concealment, hypocrisy, duplicity and the suspension of disbelief for that very reason. The integral self which does not perform is, however, a pure myth. Moreover, Goffman's unfortunate nominalist conceits detract from his historical insight, namely that Western societies have recently *become* very performative. Here we have to add to the impression-management of persons as sellers and producers the increasingly rich and varied performances of persons as consumers. Goffman's analysis of the performative forms of life made sense not *sub specie aeternitas* as he imagined, but in the cultural context of his own world and particularly his own country.

There is an uncanny parallel here between Goffman's first book *The Presentation of Self in Everyday Life* and *Godot*, Beckett's first major play. Beckett's play is remote and rural yet somehow fixes the tragicomedy of the modern city which follows it. Many of Goffman's case studies of self-presentation came from tourism in the Shetlands but his remote hotels of the 1940s point forward to the performing consumer cultures of the metropolitan heartland. What Goffman indicates is not just the greater rewards accorded to good impression-management but to the increasing replacement of myth and ritual by performance in modern culture. The irony is that his anthropological training had directed him to those forms of ritual in modern life he felt to be wrongly neglected by sociology.

But in fact they are often not forms of ritual at all. They are existential conventions, unwritten ground rules invented for often fleeting contacts, a paradox which he makes central through his dramaturgical metaphors of performance. The ability to perform increasingly carries off the fleeting encounter. More and more it has a surplus value in the affairs of daily life.

This leads us to an unappetising truth about the theatre. Its theatricality is no longer as distinct from rite or spectacle as previously imagined. The decline of rite and spectacle in the modern world has been offset, culturally, by an increase in everyday theatricality, in the importance of a theatrical ability to perform in daily life. Performance has exploded in cultural forms outside the theatre, in forms which have rivalled it and then passed it by. For despite the theatre's undoubted expansion, despite its greater variations in style and staging, its flair for taking itself out into the streets, it has been swamped since mid-century by the spectacular growth of an electronic culture. Electronic music stages its own spectaculars in open arenas. Film, radio and television enable us to hear and see 'live' events and 'live' performances. Even their documentary coverage is a 'staging' of events with its own evolving forms of theatricality. In an audio-visual culture of this kind, participants are encouraged to perform by the spectacularity of performers, the performers they in fact 'consume', like rock fans at heavy metal concerts of the seventies simultaneously performing the tune they are witnessing on cardboard guitars. Moreover, with the ubiquitous presence of sound systems, microphones and cameras, spectators are encouraged to perform in 'like' contexts elsewhere. Without media attention, they can imitate the theatrical display of emotion witnessed through one electronic medium or another. Here the exaggerated theatricalities of daily life become similar to that of performing in front of a near-empty auditorium. For we are now living, as Williams has noted, in a dramatised society.[22] Yet the new forms which allow us and encourage us to perform do not simultaneously structure our actions in the way of ritual or myth. In the manufactured melodramas of televised sport or broadcast news, ceremonies of performance are existential, not religious. As the surplus value of the event or the game, they are the icing on the cake.

The paradox is often grotesque. Vast electronic means are at our disposal but the rationale for their use is seldom clear. Nonetheless our experience of spectacle is more intense than ever, and the ideological pressure on electronic spectacle to be intense in order to sustain audiences leads to something new. Spectacle is something both acted and witnessed and acted again by its imitators in imitation of their witnessing. It is a dramatised world with which stage drama cannot hope to compete but which, equally, it can never ignore. The increase since 1968 in 'alternative' theatre is paralleled by the increase in the absorption of alternative spectacle. The cult of the performing self is part of a cultural explosion in which mass consumption and electronic media play an integral role. As an example we can take the increasing theatricality of politics. As television turns politics into instant theatre electoral campaigning aims its effect at television audiences for which its public audiences now serve as a pseudo-democratic pretext. In ironic inversion of the dialectic of appearance and reality, the democratic public becomes the superficial audience while the passive viewer becomes the real one. Drama as live spectacle is now embedded in just such a culture dominated by electronic spectacle while in a macabre gloss on the 'terror' of modernism, international terrorists stage para-theatrical outrages, spectacles of hijacking, kidnapping, bombing and murder for consumption by the news media to make their cause constantly visible to the world. Meanwhile their state enemies attempt to limit such coverage then use the same media to vilify and denounce them.

New permutations for the presentation of self are more varied than ever. This is not just the banal consequence of an expanding 'service' economy but of its iconic and cultural celebration. Increasingly television, radio, pop video, modelling, advertising and professional sport celebrate their gratification of the needs they have created in their audiences. Consumption is not only performed but is something in turn that has been previously activated by performance commodified as a need every consumer demands. Its cultural celebrations are part of the myth of 'post-industrial' society, of a society which downplays the elements of internalised conscience in the work ethic on which it still depends but extols the joys of success, competition and victory over others. More and more the ability to perform involves not only skill but hyperactive showmanship, audience impact and staged psychodrama. One of the basic premises of the counter-culture of 'sixty-eight, the spontaneous 'situation', has been quickly absorbed into the mainstream of cultural spectacle, where spontaneity is something rehearsed and performed for mass audiences. As the electronic eye transmits its visual image simultaneously to millions, audiences in turn develop new expectations of performance, new raptures of approval, new lamentations of failure, new celebrations of victory. For performer and spectator alike, all involve new forms of the audio-visual accounting of self.

Seen in this light, the ludism of tragicomedy is no eccentric pathology, but a forerunner and reluctant accomplice who fails to comply. It takes historic issue with the culture of mass perform-ance. For Lasch the performing self is the key to the new 'me-generation' of the last twenty years which celebrates the decline of genuine social engagement through a culture of narcissism.[23] The key to such a culture is the Self's inability to recognise the Other except through the game, where the Other is largely defined as a potential extension of self. The narcissistic personality lacks spatial definition, but equally temporal perspective. Hence we find a close, at times uncanny parallel between ludic disrecognising and the convenience of the world at hand. The performing self sees that world as an eternal present without future or history, a pathology which consumer culture reinforces. As the decline of the Hollywood Western has shown, the past is no longer amenable as moral myth. Myth increasingly functions only in the recent past, and then as nostalgia. Lasch points very precisely to this new frailty of the past. 'To the performing self,' he writes, 'the only reality is the identity he can construct out of the materials furnished by advertising and by mass culture, themes of popular film and fiction, and fragments torn from a vast range of cultural traditions, all of them contemporaneous to the contemporaneous mind.'[24]

In this light the disrecognitions of *Godot* are not passing aberra-tions, or mere genuflections of the 'absurd'. From a nodal point of dereliction, of a desolate *lack* of commodities, *Godot* prophetically mimics a consumer society in the making, taking the distorted mirror-image it has made of it onto the plane of the three-dimensional stage. Equally *Godot*'s modernist revival of the apo-calypse stands as an oblique prophecy of a new West and a nuclear age. Here the apocalyptic strain of tragicomedy, which runs through *Endgame*, *Icarus's Mother* and *End of the World*, fills out the loss of the past with the loss of the future. The fear of universal destruction, diffused and repressed into a sense of running out of time, has narrowed the contours of time itself. Living for the present is the cult of a dystopian amnesia in which the present as primal anxiety claws its way forwards and backwards in blind panic, recognising no other time but its own. In tragicomedy the separate refrains of the narcissistic and the nuclear find unexpected harmony. Lasch's diagnosis echoes the tragicomic pathos of lost identities, boundaries blurred between Self and Other, history disappearing in the fudged contours of inadequate definition. But he could also have added the fear of the future that is largely repressed beneath the sanitised sanity of public discourse.

It is significant that in his discourse on performance Lasch is perceptive about everything except the theatre. He falsely takes what he calls 'absurd theatre' as a symptom of the malaise he diagnoses, as evidence rather than insight, disease rather than vision. In short, trapped within the subjectivist prism of absurdity, ludism languishes as a sign of the rot that is about to set in. But tragicomedy with its precise limits upon empathy gives itself an aesthetic distance from the pathologies it uncovers. Its intricate play on play endows it with structures of feeling which take it beyond the phenomenology of absurd experience. There is something more universal here than the Americanised focus on bourgeois narcissism now open to all, as 'classless', through the commodifications of consumer culture. Tragicomedy is a world of lack which glosses a world of abundance, a world of obscurity which glosses a world of eminence. Here it observes a double dialectic. Its culturally derelict inhabitants are excluded both from the world of rationalised control and the world of performative eminence. They possess neither mastery nor recognition in the broader fabric of society. Instead they are vulnerable through what they do not know, what they cannot control, through the participation in the game that is not their own. Stoppard's *Rosenkrantz and Guildenstern are Dead* formalises this conceit by turning the tragedy of the noble Prince of Denmark into a tragicomedy of bemused courtiers modelled on Didi and Gogo who are caught up in the intricacies of an intrigue they do not understand. Tragicomedy's modern protagonists by contrast work best when they are excluded from control and from fame. The major exception to the latter is Shepard's *The Tooth of Crime* whose two central figures have neither the resources to resist fame nor to survive it, and whose identities are eventually consumed by the consumer culture in which they are willingly but helplessly immersed. And fame itself is ruthlessly deconstructed by Genet in *The Balcony* when revolutionary crisis entails that images of the famous persist only through *ad hoc* impersonations by nonentities.

The danger signals for tragicomedy lie in the temptations of didacticism or of *embourgeoisement*. One finds something of a problematic movement in Pinter from *The Homecoming* to *Old Times* and *No Man's Land*, but more so in Bond from *Saved* to *The Sea*, in Albee from *The Zoo Story* to *Tiny Alice*, in Stoppard from *Jumpers* to *Night and Day* and *The Real Thing*, and in Shepard from *Fool for Love* to *A Lie of the Mind*. If play and performance lose their edge of desperation, if they can be reduced to the level of an intricate game over which there finally *is* control, then they lose their relationship to fate. Disrecognising loses its crucial edge. The shocks of disrecognition must always be embellished by the shock value of familiar objects. In place of *Godot*'s empty stage, Pinter and Shepard find a menace in the ordinary. The cheese sandwich in *The Homecoming* and the refrigerator in *Curse of the Starving Class* are neutral, metonymic objects given a comic and chilling force. Their power comes from being more than what we could imagine, repositories of a surplus value which surprises us. They constantly mean more than they should. By doing so, they mean less and less what they originally were.

This movement away from the metasocial world of dramatic realism confronts us with a paradox. In disrupting familiar meanings, play and disrecognising often transform objects that are known into things that are strange. Through their display of things near at hand, things familiar, the new dramatic structures trade on the menace of the unknown, of something unnervingly beyond obvious motive or clear appearance. This, above all, has been Beckett's legacy. The onus on modernist spectators is to work out why familiar objects are so menacing and so strange. They have to translate back that strangeness, as a performed disguise of the metonymic, into something they truly recognise, knowing there is no complete translation. Bemused, shocked and inspired, they have to know they are searching for the missing pieces to complete the jigsaw. They also have to know that the pieces will never be found and the puzzle never solved. Contemporary tragicomedy has thrust the dramatic masking and re-presentation of social facts into a spiral of uncertainty. Its forceful gestures towards social reality are undercut by the absence of any guarantee of the authentic experience of the Real. That historical movement and its intricate detail, from Beckett to Shepard, now remain to be charted.

3
The Resistance of Commodities

Play and disrecognising are not merely forms of modernist rupture. Their continuity with earlier structures of feeling is equally vital. Here we can trace their emergence out of the dominant structures of liberal tragedy Williams has analysed from Ibsen onwards.[1] These can be seen as complex structures of guilt and imprisonment, where a conscience-stricken hero succumbs as victim to a constraining environment. Williams notes that the naturalist trap of the three-walled room has its origins in romantic melodrama, in the imprisonment placed upon the romantic hero he must cast aside in order to escape and triumph. On Ibsen's stage such romantic possibilities of triumph are remote. Confinement is usually unending and intolerable. But in addition to that Ibsenist confinement which entices our sympathy are forms of strangeness which puzzle us, a sense of place which is off-centre or peripheral and can make us lose our cultural bearings. We can note the abyss of nature to be found in *Little Eyolf* and *John Gabriel Borkman*, or Ibsen's mocking references to the demonic trolls of folk legend. There is the strange attic sheltering the wounded pet in *The Wild Duck*, or the harsh 'nobility' of lineage claimed by John Rosmer and Hedda Gabler. All these confound our idea of naturalism as 'natural' happening, as the faithful reproduction of the normal event. Instead they subvert empathy through their strange and estranged socio-spatial forms. Ibsen is never natural. He is a constant culture-shock.

Such culture-shock has profound implications for dramatic realism. In Synge, Lorca, O'Casey and O'Neill, subjective moods of alienation are matched by objective alienation-effects, by extremes of class and remote location. *Riders to the Sea* and *Blood Wedding* offer us worlds of adversity beyond civilisation. *The Plough and the Stars* and *The Iceman Cometh* show us the hidden interiors of the underclass in the modern city. Audience sympathy is qualified by cultural distance, by the sense of seeing something unnerving and strange. This, it is true, helps to expose empathy as an often tired convention of bourgeois drama. But the crucial factor is the variation in distance, the way we fluctuate between sympathy and resistance. Ibsen invites us to feel compassion for his tragic heroes only to confront us with the calculated savagery of Hedda's destructive wishes or the near-Hitlerian insanity of Borkman. In O'Neill's *Iceman*, Hickey the salesman-evangelist descends against all expectation into a dark void and we refuse to follow, even though at first we find him more normal than his drunken disciples. All this Williams underestimates. So it needs to be reasserted. The stylistic alienation-effects of modern tragedy, which link Ibsen to Brecht, feed in dramatic realism off thematic alienations of character. The topography of such alienation, its peripheral setting, means that environment is never totally constraining. There is always the chance of resistance to compromise, and of knowing one has actively made the wrong choice. Hedda Gabler, John Rosmer and Rebecca West sense they have made the wrong choice. Their suicides are no mere capitulation, but acts of self-punishment which are also acts of defiance. They are a response to the paradox of being estranged from the world and trapped by it at the same time. As a response to that paradox, their actions are both perverse and moral. Within such complex ambiguity lies the sense of their tragic heroism.

In tragicomedy this is no longer possible. The structures of feeling have been transformed. The self is in a vacuum and knows no morality. Suicide will never happen. Instead of alienation we have failures to recognise. Instead of naturalistic constraint we have a contained playfulness. The changes may be less than absolute, but they are still vital. The forgettings of the frail persona replace the estrangements of the perverse but moral hero. Failures of memory and naming damage even further the damaged self. Play, meanwhile, is the ludic enhancement of the stage-as-prison. In Beckett and Soyinka it can turn the naturalist trap of the walled room into the ontological trap of the open road. The trap, once natural and domestic, is now without obvious boundary. Yet Vladimir and Estragon can no more move from the stage when intent demands it than the barflies in Harry Hope's saloon. At the end they do not move. In *Endgame* Hamm is confined to the sofa on castors that is his throne just as Hedda is trapped into a diet of dreary piano recitals. There is, however, a vital difference. In Ibsen and O'Neill there are clear exits. To leave has a meaning. In Beckett and Genet there is a constant playing with exits but no meaningful exit at all.

After O'Neill, tragedy begins to weaken. In *Cat on a Hot Tin Roof*, *Death of a Salesman* and *Look Back in Anger* it narrowly averts a cloying mix of guilt and capitulation. Elsewhere it brims over into sentimental melodrama. The spectator is often too close to hero-victims who fail to conceal their own failures, hero-victims trying to resist injustice by blaming others who in turn become the victims of the victim. Willy Loman transfers his guilt and sense of failure onto his family, trying to make *them* feel guilty for *his* inadequacy. At a broad tangent to the realist stage and this crisis of feeling, Beckett and Genet seem to provide a way out. They release us from the suffocations of the flayed conscience. Play is in the ascendency. But play's comic and caustic confusions also challenge the psychological conventions of the Real. The tragicomic persona is no longer a knowing person immersed in the dilemmas of conscience, but stays helplessly anchored beneath that threshold of knowledge on which conscience is based. So baffled and bemused are ludic heroes by the nature of the world in which they live that the ontological conditions for justice do not even exist. In realism, justice is signposted in order that it may be evaded. But in tragicomedy the capacity to distinguish right and wrong barely seems to exist.

This moral failure shades over into disrecognising. There is an apt comparison here between O'Neill and Beckett. The audience sees Mary Tyrone's inner retreat as a gradual loss of the power of judgement. Like the other Tyrones we come to await her entrances with bated breath, confronted by a modern middle-aged Ophelia. In so doing, we share their distress and compassion. In *Godot*, on the other hand, the return of Pozzo and Lucky in the second act permits no consensus between Didi and Gogo and their audience. The audience still do not know who Didi and Gogo are while the hapless pair in turn cannot identify the intruders. In O'Neill we see Mary's loss of judgement through the sane gaze of her flawed family. But we cannot really 'see' anything through Didi and Gogo. Instead of sharing their bated breath as they watch, we watch their baffled watching with amused bafflement. They cannot mediate our gaze. While O'Neill shows us conscience through the gaze, Beckett shows us a dark yet comic confusion where little conscience exists. The audience is left out in the cold.

From Ibsen onwards conscience has been engaged by the

revelation of social horrors at first concealed from view. Mary Tyrone's morphine addiction or Oswald's syphilis work as devices of the unspoken finally revealed. By contrast, in Sam Shepard's tragicomedies of the narcotic age, the isolated case of addiction or horror is no longer a fatal weakness, a moral nightmare to be concealed and then dramatically unloaded. Instead we witness polar extremes. On the one hand, there is the open and ritual 'shooting up' of Hoss by his doctor in *The Tooth of Crime*. On the other hand we have nothing explicit at all. That 'nothing at all', however, suggests the invisible presence of narcotics in most of Shepard's plays. To use one of his own titles, it often works like the 'unseen hand', an invisible arbiter of fate. Much of the time his characters will talk and act like part-time solipsists, high or hallucinating. Yet the dialogue gives no direct clues, the action no direct evidence. Shepard's world shows us trance without the needle or the pouch, ineffable yet colouring the whole texture of the stage experience. In its paranoia and its desperations, we see the effect but not the cause. Formally absent, we uncannily sense it to be 'there'. Unlike the conspicuous drinking of Weston in *Curse of the Starving Class*, its invisible aura pervades the extended inactions of *Action*, one of the most important of Shepard's plays. Because Mary Tyrone's narcotic reverie is part of a visible, climactic journey into night, there is still a contrast with the light of day. But in Shepard dreams and drugs, day and night, reality and fantasy become inseparable.

In modern tragedy, the alien is often based on spatial exclusion. Ibsen, Chekhov, Synge and Lorca centre their action on peripheries of nation and culture, country and civilisation. Their settings often seem to exist on the *edge* of nowhere, between civilisation and wilderness. Their characters seem uncannily misplaced, as if civilisation were always somewhere else, a function of impassable or impossible distance. In a single image it is the distance of Chekhov's three sisters from their beloved Moscow. Scenic exclusion in tragicomedy is rather different. It returns closer to the centres of civilisation but at times evokes no immediate sense of place. It tends to situate its exclusions in the *middle* of nowhere, in a setting where what is beyond the stage cannot readily be visualised. Often, despite precise stage directions, the setting is elusive, or seems to be surrounded by vacancy. While it is possible to see the landscapes of fiord and forest through the open doors of Ibsen's rooms, or be taken outside by Chekhov through the changing of the acts, tragicomedy uncannily blunts the naturalistic imagining of exteriors. Minimal evoking is a shock effect. The ramshackle flat of *The Caretaker* suggests no more what is outside than the open road of *Godot* suggests what lies beyond. There is no outlook, only as in *Endgame* or *Buried Child* nightmarish reports of the outside, a claustrophobic, chronicled vision of what the audience never sees. We do not imagine a wider community beyond the stage.

In the families of Pinter and Shepard one finds consequently a major contrast with the families of Miller or O'Neill. They seem to have no neighbours, or be part of any neighbourhood or community. They are largely isolated and implosive from the outset. Their visitors are outsiders, to be feared and mistrusted. Apart from such unwelcome intrusions into their domestic space the world, it seems, passes them by. They are insignificant or forgotten, not part of any collective life. They lack the power of connection. It is easy to see why tragicomedy then becomes a drama of pawns rather than pieces. Knowledge and power lie elsewhere. So does morality. By failing to understand themselves and the world in any absolute sense, the inhabitants of the tragicomic stage seem doomed to an existence without recognisable values. The subject of tragic drama becomes the tragicomic object, an unempathic object of the spectator's gaze, part of the desultory landscape and furniture of a commodified world. Such human 'objects' blend with the boots on their feet or the empty refrigerators in their kitchen. They are cartoon heroes sprung loose from the strip on the page, their tragic pathos embroiled in monstrous comedies of error. This is storyboard drama, not so much of the downtrodden as the forgotten, a drama of nonentities.

Their fate is oblique because they seem to us to be subterraneans, to be sub-natural. They are not, as Nietzsche prophesied, beyond good and evil. Rather they are *beneath* good and evil. If God is dead, then no one has replaced Him, and certainly not them. To be unknown, to be anonymous, is not only to lack the watchful gaze of the Almighty, but also that of the ruling class. It is to be someone of no importance. That is why the play of tragicomedy appears to have no grand design, why it appears as a structure without structures, a series of random gains and losses on the edge of the abyss. In such unstructured games the players are like pawns unwittingly moving themselves in the wrong direction. Such pawns cannot stand in for conscience, guilt and compassion.

Instead they are aleatory signs of misdirection or confusion. But in critical discourse this has led to a different kind of confusion. The modish delight in *jouissance* is not, as it imagines, a liberation from the darker structures of modernism which it claims to repudiate. It is often a transparent and *post hoc* celebration of this randomness of play, a randomness which has its origin in Beckett and Genet, where it is theatre and not pedantry, performance and not idle speculation, darkness as much as pleasure. So-called 'post-modern' play is an easy utopia only because it overlooks this formidable dystopian power. What was originally gesture and image, body and sign, has congealed into the pedant's cult of *la langue*. But tragicomedy still thrives without it. For play as pure language, as paraliterary text and not performance, is an illusion which betrays a total ignorance of theatre.

The culture of exclusion cannot be reduced to any obvious hierarchy of classes, but it still invokes the whole nature of power. It embraces failed domination just as much as the equality of the subjugated. In *The Maids*, Madame's lover, the absent despot, is an indifferent pimp about to be arrested for trivial crimes. In act two of *Godot* the blind Pozzo becomes on one version the apotheosis of the Anglo-Irish Descendancy and on another, a bedraggled Gaulei-ter retreating from Occupied France with his racially subhuman slave. Certainly there is reversal of fortune, but here and in *Endgame*, Beckett seems to explore the nadir of power without ever showing its zenith. In *The Homecoming*, *Curse of the Starving Class* and *Buried Child* the official heads of household, all male, are eunuchs in the real world of power. They shout all the louder for being baffled to distraction, and are toppled from a stool rather than a pedestal. The excluded have their own frail hierarchies which, without their knowing or wishing it, produce a travesty of the rational world from which they are excluded. And they too are travesties. Their bewilderment mocks the whole idea of authority since they in effect authorise nothing and are themselves never legitimate.

Their disobedient underlings become the victimised objects of those who, lacking legitimacy, appear as victims themselves. Pozzo becomes blind, while Max in *The Homecoming*, Dodge in *Buried Child*, and Weston in *Curse of the Starving Class* find they have the power to order nothing in their own house. Shepard's heroes seem to spend their time failing to identify the house they are living in. Diminished patriarchy here differs markedly from the realism of

Miller or Williams which points to a possible rational authority. In *Streetcar* the contained power of Stanley Kowalski is turned inward. Sexual power over Stella and Blanche may compensate for lack of class power but the Napoleonic code of Louisiana is something Kowalski can follow, even for his own purposes. Tragicomedy, by contrast, lacks external models of rationality and so undermines the dramatic space of male power. Lack of power on the outside is matched by lack of power on the inside. Shepard's unreliable fathers cannot even make the connections between the two. They can no more control the household than they can resist the hostile world which threatens it. Absence of good and evil, of conscience and the law, rather than their guilty betrayal becomes the typical fate of the excluded. Exclusion is not just exclusion from the world of privilege, but also from the world of reason.

Weakened authority clashes comically with fantasies of power, most of which never come to fruition. In Genet such fantasy is explosive. It triggers all his dazzling role-transformations, maid and mistress in *The Maids*, nonentity and oppressor in *The Balcony*, colonial subject and white ruler in *The Blacks*. In Soyinka it goes further with the renegade dictators and diplomatic acolytes of *A Play of Giants*. In Shepard it goes further with the toppling of Hoss by Crow in *The Tooth of Crime*, the role-switching of Lee and Austin in *True West*, the green facial slime a demented Rabbit inherits from the deposed Wheeler in *Angel City*. In Genet reversal has the measured purity of illusion enveloping the supreme desire for domination. In Soyinka sudden loss of power is a comic yet horrifying charade. In Shepard, at the heart of the nightmare of the American Dream, the inversions are more functions of role than of character. The alacrity of the sudden switch, matching modernism to the themes of American melodrama, is balanced by a social hierarchy which entails rise and fall, the outsider moving in and upward, the insider moving down and out. Positions change on the wheel of fortune but the wheel of fortune remains itself unchanged. Roles become transferable labels and performance turns them inside out.

What we find here is not the indifference to character both Genet and Shepard have professed. It is a radically different conception of character, one which abandons the quest in *Strange Interlude* for psychic depth or the Expressionist concern with the cosmic mysteries of the soul. Tragicomedy also works at a tangent from the modernist novel which so often abandoned the external description of characters in favour of a language of the different levels of human consciousness. But if it reduces our concern with mental interiors, it enhances our concern with the performance of self. The tragicomic hero may be culturally and mentally impoverished but it is a poverty enriched by performance. Character is defined by expression, by play, by the supercharged role adopted in a particular game. It depends crucially on performance. The hyperactive performer atones for the poverty of culture and the poverty of self. At one level, a tragicomic persona is the representation of the reduced person in the age of modernity, neither concerned citizen nor pillar of the community but a nobody who appears to lack powers of reasoning and judgement. Yet hyperactive performance is also unofficial citizenship, alternative identity. If the persona of a character is reduced to that of a mere role then the character takes that role into another dimension. The impulse to perform is the impulse to transcend exclusion. In tragicomedy elevation to the level of performance is the form theatrical resistance takes to the plight of degradation. Thirty years after *Godot*, the growing underclass of Western societies takes up its own threatening forms of theatricality on the streets, while terrorists take theirs up anywhere and everywhere.

Modern philosophy suggests another dimension to exclusion. In performative culture the Sartrean 'project' which informs the futurity of all rational beings is never fully grounded. The projecting of action forward, that is, into the long-term future, is severed from the contradictory intentions of the situation at hand. In Pinter we can see the use of this as a dramatic strategy. In Ruth's shock acceptance of the unforeseen invitation at the end of *The Homecoming* we have a challenge to our sense that she must surely turn back eventually to the needs of her own family. Her 'motivation' for not doing so is never made clear. The decision challenges our idea of what planning in that instance must be, our idea that despite transient aberration we always return to normal futures. Pinter makes the point even more tellingly by turning the aberration into an alternative plan for the future. Ruth's decision to 'swap' families is a future plan which travesties the future. It puts us on the spot because it does not seem that it could be part of any rational plan. It appears at first that she is merely selling herself into slavery, or more strictly, fantasy. But Pinter forces us through this rupture with reason and futurity into seeing how she can invent a counter-plan to dominate her male dominators. In the second act of the play switches of intent are bewildering, aleatory, alarming travesties of those wider conceptions of project which define selfhood in daily life, reason in philosophy and character in fiction.[2] In general disrecognising hives off memory from a person's identity. Rational failures to project forward sever intention from futurity. The moral agency of rational purpose becomes a gaping hole rent in the flimsy costume of the ludic persona.

Tragicomedy is not totally a drama of exclusion. Exclusions from culture and power are powerfully balanced by *inclusions* through language. The language of a debased public discourse speaks *through* the socially excluded figures of Orton, Pinter, Mamet and Shepard. It sets limits to their powers of speech. It is the language of occlusion and evasion, outdated custom and current cliché. The language is often used inventively – witness the sales talk in *Glengarry Glen Ross*. But the language is always something given, imposed. It is something from the outside, a cross the ludic persona has to bear. Inclusion means to be trapped within its limits, and at times, to be trapped *by* its limits. The inventiveness of the spoken word, the quick retort, the skilful silence, the ruthless put-down are countermanded by the limits of the language itself. The kings and queens of the telling phrase become, at a stroke, the comic pawns of language games they never created. These invariably trap them into speaking in a certain way just as game-playing traps them into acting in a certain way. After Beckett, they are dramatised as commodified beings in an epoch of consumer commodities. Their exclusions set them apart from 'normal' consumers, isolated, culturally denuded, out on a limb. But their inclusion through spoken language, through ludic dialogue, sets them out as marker-buoys of the commodified world. Tragicomedy, in that sense, parallels the 'making strange' of the cultural object which the human subject has become in a society of mass consumption.

This is not to say tragicomedians do not have their own language, their own way of talking. Nor is it to say that they cannot use language as a source of terror or power. They often do and with chilling results. They are supremely inventive, one might say, in the use of a language which is ultimately not their own, which sells them short in its failures to connect just as much as it deludes them in their bid to wield power. They are supreme counterfeiters of a debased coinage. They are so precisely because they *are* outsiders. This strange dialectic of excluded inclusion marks off tragicomedy from earlier structures of alienation but also from contemporary fictions of the reified subject in, for example, the *nouveau roman*. Its inclusions through language make its characters incapable of tragic alienation. Their social exclusions, however, prevent instant saturation by a reified world. They have pretensions without conscience and destinies devoid of rational explanation. But they are not yet commodified subjects, not yet things because of the vital link between performance and exclusion.

As comedians they hold themselves at arm's length from complete absorption. This gives tragicomedy its uneasy place in contemporary art and culture. Its dramatic form is a modernist departure from the Real but equally a modernist resistance to the closures of the 'post-modern' which, according to its proponents, collapses the boundaries between consumption and art. Play and disrecognising are resolute defiances of this closure. Moreover, Beckett and Genet are part of a modernist renaissance and their tragicomedy shows important continuities in the divided modernism of this century. It renews the apocalyptic strains of Expressionism, but in a cooler, less intense form. It sustains the Imagist concentration on the sparse, clear detail of the instant in time but suspends the cyclical eruptions of myth and allusion. It is central to modernism but also demonstrates a curious hiatus, a strange Return in which tragicomedy breaks with its High Modernist ancestors, in which it takes two steps forward by taking one step backward.

Anderson succinctly places this break by suggesting three historical coordinates of the original 'modernist conjuncture'.[3] The first was a rejection of the formalised academicism of the *ancien régime* against which it was easy for avant-gardes to protest, the second was the new communicative technologies of a second industrial revolution – telephone, radio, cars and planes – about which it was easy to become either gloomy or elated, and the third was the proximity of social revolution in continental Europe from which no one could hide. This triadic relationship of iconoclasm, technological transformation and revolutionary change is complex but vital. It sustains a fragmented and heterogeneous modernism, a set of modernisms, but also, as Wyndham Lewis stressed, it sets in process changes which drive them quickly towards exhaustion.[4] While modernism found little nourishment in Britain in the stable and still deeply conservative society which existed after 1926, in continental Europe it became the victim of political reaction, cut down brutally in Hitler's Germany and Stalin's Russia, curtailed in Austria, Italy and Spain. Postponed by the Second World War, it was postponed further by the Stalinisation of Eastern Europe and the emergence of the Cold War thereafter. Equally it is only after the war in the West has finished that modernism overcomes its cultural exhaustion and gains a second lease of life.

The second wave of modernism, which begins in the middle of the fifties, is accelerated by a weakening of cultural censorship towards which it contributes in no small measure, and the wider movement towards mass consumption and modest affluence in the revitalised economies of the West. Beckett and Genet are at the heart of its revival in the theatre. A further catalyst is the creation of a new professional intelligentsia through higher education which increases rapidly right through the sixties until the explosion of 'sixty-eight' and beyond. But all these developments took place within the context of the Cold War and the fear of nuclear war. The historical situation was very different from the end of the First World War. Instead of the proximity of revolution, there was the proximity of Stalinist pseudo-revolution. Communicative technologies advanced rapidly, but within the context of a globally destructive defence system to which they make no small contribution. The deferential domestic-servant class which serviced a genteel upper-middle class and a now largely defunct aristocracy was gradually replaced by the depersonalised service-class of a corporate service economy which is meant to 'service' everyone, though never of course equally. It is mistaken to see this coexistence of the Cold War and consumerism as inimical to modernism. Jameson, in particular, is wrong to argue for a pervasive collapse of the tensions between post-war art and the new forms of consumer capitalism.[5] What has happened is rather different. The revolutionary avant-gardes of early modernism never reappeared, but the *myth* of the avant-garde very clearly did. For, as everyone knew, the earlier modernist aesthetic forged out of painting, cinema and theatre had been in deep conflict with modernity. The myth of the avant-garde was vital to the reawakening of modernism but its flair for the shock of the new, especially in those groups who self-consciously proclaimed themselves as innovators, has been more prone to commodification than to revolution. Tragicomedy too differed from its modernist predecessors. High Modernism paralleled Einsteinian theory in destroying the fixity of the empirical world – in making us aware all that was solid appeared to melt into air.[6] At the same time as it attempted to parallel the bewildering experience of modernity, however, it also attempted to transcend modernity through a unified aesthetic of myth, time, future and memory. In the tragicomic, this unity breaks down. Indeed it is never even attempted.

In the second wave of modernism, tragicomedy is as integral to film as it is to drama. As early as 1940 Renoir had suggested its possibilities in *La Règle du Jeu* with its sudden breathtaking changes of mood, from joy to melancholy, elegance to awkwardness, from sordid farce to violent death. He breaches the classic 'rules of the game' in which masters and servants interact but have separate destinies not only by lyrically interweaving them but by giving them a tragic destiny. He also proved that it was entirely cinematic to alter mood within the single shot or sequence. The emergence of the long take and the mobile camera were essential aids to such lyric transitions of mood, to the coexistence of tragic and comic forms. This was to prove equally true of Welles' *Touch of Evil*, Godard's *Breathless*, Truffaut's *Jules and Jim*, Raffelson's *Five Easy Pieces*, Wenders' *Kings of the Road* and Terence Malick's *Badlands*. The long take, the tracking shot, the jump cut and the voice-over are lyrical alienation-effects, distancing mechanisms which efface empathy and diminish character. Welles's grotesque Hank Quinlan suggests the inflated ruling effigies of Genet's *Balcony*, all impotent patriarchs. The Belmondo persona Godard creates in *Breathless* and *Pierrot le Fou* is a tragedian of the cartoon strip, a hyperactive outlaw devoid of certainty or values, vainly searching for passion and communication and finding only a numb destruction. The one certainty in a world of male grotesques and women he can only talk past rather than to is death. In *Pierrot* and in *Jules and Jim* suicide is a tragic instant, a sudden change of mood, but not, in essence, a tragic act. In *Badlands* Malick's hero-villain is the spitting image of James Dean in a memory-film which poisons American nostalgia. Moreover, he is a polite but chilling psychopath. Like many of Shepard's Western heroes, but more extreme, he craves celebrity as a path out of anonymity, a cartoon figure incapable of judging the consequences of his own actions. In Malick's skilful dislocation of sound and image the naive voice-over of the romantic teenage girlfriend turns the violent mayhem into tragicomic farce.

In all these instances the heroic is not an agonising of conscience under adverse conditions but the struggle of the excluded to resist inclusion, of diminished selves who reject, albeit comically, a commodified world, to refuse to become machines. It is a different world from that of Bergman, Bresson, Resnais and Antonioni who look more seriously to the social and psychic dilemmas of the European bourgeoisie, and who take on in cinematic form the legacy of Proust and Mann, Fitzgerald and Woolf. Here psychic estrangement is the dominant mood, an ontological given, above all a *female* point of view. Reified landscapes become visual landscapes of mind and the camera lingers on the petrified image, the anxious gaze. Any sudden change of mood would destroy that landscape and its aesthetic. It is prepared at times not to be lyrical in order not to be whimsical. By contrast, the French New Wave is prepared to be whimsical in order to be lyrical. Here the sudden and lyric change of mood is the New Wave version of tragicomedy, of the disrecognitions and role-reversals of the modernist stage. Volatile and unpredictable, their ignoble heroes make a farce out of tragedy and comedy out of their own absurd pretensions.

In neither theatre nor cinema of this period is there evidence of the 'post-modern' elision of art and consumption. Instead they are parallel innovations in the modernist aesthetic. In neither case is the human subject merely reified as object, but equally in neither case is the human subject a centred 'individual'. In tragicomedy the staging of strangeness, the dramatising of exclusion pre-empts the reified and triumphs in its shock resistances to the commodified world. We see an alien world that is somehow familiar, that is ours and not ours. We see the casualties of our world in their intransitive habitus, neither totally estranged nor totally commodified. The ludic stage does not yield like a bankrupt modernism to the plastic blandishments of the 'post-modern' – 'one void chasing another', as Anderson puts it. Instead it consolidates, like film, a new stage in its relationship to modernity. It may now be that the age of tragicomedy has passed. The latest work of Pinter, Mamet and Shepard, as well as the last decade of the cinema, would seem to testify to that. In the next century it may seem no more than a brief coda to modern tragedy. Alternatively it may be seen as a key feature of the modernist art of the Anglo-American world. More widely it could be seen to dominate all drama in the English language. Only time will tell.

It does not of course dominate the modernist tradition as a whole. The legacy of Brecht and Piscator has produced a more consciously political theatre in the neo-modernist period, the work of Frisch, Dürennmatt, Grass, Peter Weiss and Heiner Müller in Germany, the work of Bond, Arden, Hare, Hampton, Edgar and Brenton in Britain. It may also be part of a *belated* modernism in the Anglo-American scheme of things, with Pinter, Orton and Stoppard compensating for the lack of an English Joyce earlier in the century, just as Bond, Hare and Brenton seem to compensate for the lack of an English Brecht. In the United States, the experimental excesses of the sixties often seem like a pallid and belated avant-gardism to compensate for the absence of any theatre in that country, despite O'Neill, to make a sustained response to the modernist eruptions in Europe after the First World War. Throughout this period there is always a process of catching up that takes place on the English language stage, an overdue compensation for the gaps in its own history. On the evidence of the last three decades it has at the very least drawn abreast of the modernist challenge. In that respect it owes no small debt to the work of Samuel Beckett.

4

Samuel Beckett:
Imprisoned Persona and
Irish Amnesia

The fashionable notion of Beckett's writing as a coherent unity is a myth. His first published novel, *Murphy*, with its archaic Johnsonian syntax and collapsing sentence structures, is a mixture of juvenile melancholia and sub-Joycean humour which never finally works. His further adventures into the sustained narrative of depressive psychosis, *Watt*, *Malone Dies* and *Molloy* are a major advance but still grapple despairingly with the problematic of narrative entropy. In writing fiction Beckett often produced stage Irishmen in disguise. In writing plays he projected his Irish heritage onto a universal plane. Like Joyce before him, necessary exile spurred him to artistic greatness. But unlike Joyce, it was not achieved by writing about the city he had left behind him. As the son of an upper-middle-class Protestant family on the outer rim of Dublin, his fiction lacked Joyce's precise and uncanny hold over the city, that masterly use of visual topography and clinching detail which pervades *Ulysses*. The city, one senses, was never his. Nor was the language. Exile entailed a mortification of the spirit through the forsaking of native language and its idiom, the curing of verbal excess by a double translation – from novel to play and from English to French, whence the actual text could be translated back again in triumph. This double exile of culture and language which Beckett found in Paris, and his puritanical resolution of it made him more of a genuine successor to Joyce and Synge than when he consciously tried to imitate them. Through the French language Beckett became one of the three great Irish dramatists of the twentieth century.

Written just after the completion of *Malone Dies* in 1949, *Waiting for Godot* translated the embryonic conceits of his intricate narrative into effective dramatic form. The overlap is indeed crucial, for Beckett evolved his dramatic devices out of narrative. If *Malone*

Dies is at times a harrowing experience, it is also a narrowing one, translating the precise sights and sounds of Joyce's Dublin into a numb and featureless no man's land. For the autobiographical figures of his fiction, the fictional versions of Beckett himself, are gradually honed down to appear as life's dying and desiccated victims, devoid of desire, sub-Proustian heroes with little or no remembrance of time past. At this level, the flayed text is lame compensation for the sterility of impotent heroes and Beckett's reader becomes a sacrificial lamb to the altar of an ascetic modernism, a masochist who accepts that his nose will be rubbed in the dust of an artistic wasteland.

Yet in narrative Beckett finds the germs of disrecognition and play which make his drama so disturbing. In his plays too it is flawed, unfinished narrative which Beckett so brilliantly dramatises. For Malone, story-telling is a form of play, a game which offers fleeting salvation from the darkness of the night. It also atones for the narrator's failure to 'play' with others in his past life. Yet that free, play-ful imagination is the imagination of a dying man who confuses the play of narrative with the play of memory. Malone being thrust without prehistory into his present room and Molloy finding himself alone in the room of his dead mother have sonorous echoes of Heidegger at his darkest. Malone does not appear to know how he got there, does not recognise the house in which he seems to have awoken and cannot remember the last thing he remembers. Not to be outdone, Molloy cannot say whether his dead mother had died prior to his arrival or after it, being totally unable to recall either event. For Malone, such failures of recognition are not unusual. He claims to have lived in a kind of coma. But he also claims the resulting loss of consciousness was never any loss.[1] At one level this is the diminutive pathos of the bourgeois Protestant child born on the outskirts of an intensely Catholic city. At another it is no kind of pathos at all since the admirer of Proust has become a calculated anti-Proust, puritanically denying to himself the quest for the magic of pure memory.

The transfer of these narrative forms to drama is nothing short of electrifying. Beckett shares with Genet the same power to resolve the problematic of fiction by changing forms. In Genet's case it is the transformation from the poetic but prurient stasis of Querelle-camp to the dramatic illusions of a sexuality which can never be finally fixed or known. In Beckett it is a transfer from the flaccid narrative of endless monologue to the dialogues of paired characters who double the split self. Here the balanced and symmetrical ciphers of dialogue are the offspring of vaudeville clowns and the great comics of the silent cinema. Yet their voices clearly speak a language of dark times amidst hilarity and confusion. Their failures of knowing and remembering are now classic features of the modernist idiom. But this kind of amnesia is also an Irish amnesia, a forgetting firmly rooted in a remembered tradition, that of the Irish theatre without which it would never have been possible.

Beckett's plays are both an extension and a rejection of his Protestant Irish predecessors.[2] His minimal language is a devastating riposte to the romantic superabundance of Yeats and Synge, to the high nobility of the former's verse drama and the poetic hyperbole in the speech of the latter's Irish peasants. Yet his spare dialogues also contain much of their succinctness and their sense of tragic loss, of catastrophe as something beyond remedy and understanding. At times, *Godot* and *Endgame* suggest variations out of *On Baile's Strand*. In *Godot* the blind man and the Fool become Didi and Gogo without the noble presence of Cuchulain – Godot never appears. Yet Pozzo, the pathetic emanation of authority without nobility who becomes blind, suggests Cuchulain's degenerate scion. *Endgame*, by contrast, has Hamm as both blind man and degenerate scion and Clov as the Fool living in a world where all nobility is extinct. With Synge's *The Well of the Saints*, the echoes of Irish drama become more pressing. Godot can be seen as a version of Synge's saint who never comes and, anyway, cannot dispense miracles. In Synge, the saint restores Martin Doul's sight, the gift of seeing which proves more painful than the affliction of blindness. In a form of disrecognising later made more familiar by Beckett, Doul's immediate error in regaining his sight is to mistake the pretty Molly Byrne for Mary, his ugly deformed wife. Blindness as necessary pathos, by which Beckett fuses the loss of the eyes with the loss of the soul, is firmly echoed in the pathos of his predecessors.

The resurrection of the 'noble' that Yeats and Synge had discovered in the Irish folk-tales of the Kings of Ulster and mythically endorsed in their own drama becomes in Beckett a lost universe. Its redemptive power as a myth of national awakening is reduced in his writing to a dim hope, a distant trace of the possible. Yet *Godot's* dramatic space simultaneously opens out its theatrical legacy. In *The Well of the Saints*, for instance, there is the open, sparsely cultivated countryside, the comic presencing of the peasant poor which *Godot* echoes in minimal form. The change of acts is also similar. In Act 1 Synge has an open roadside with a low loose wall at the back and gap in the centre. In Act 3 the gap is filled with 'briers, or branches'. In *Godot* the single tree, previously bare in Act 1, grows a handful of leaves by the start of Act 2. The difference is thematic. In Beckett there is no 'miracle' but the opposite, the onset of blindness rather than the restoration of sight. The blindness is both metaphor and reality. The blindness of the returning Pozzo glosses the 'blindness' of Didi and Gogo in never knowing for certain if they have ever seen Godot or whether indeed he has had any impact upon their past life at all. Recollection, so important in Yeats and Synge, becomes in Beckett a dimming candle that is finally snuffed. And with recollection goes redemption. Beyond the faint buried traces of Irish myth lies the waning of something more powerful, Beckett's own religiosity. The 'myth' his plays repress is not so much the 'myth' of a glorious, ancient Ireland as the myth of Christian redemption.

His radio play *All That Fall* gives an important clue to that stifled religiosity. It has more naturalist movement than most of his plays, set mainly in a suburban railway station and its surroundings with a motley ageing crew of suburban Dubliners. The atmosphere is genteel yet desperate, resonating with Protestant defensiveness and decay. Mrs Rooney who can barely drag her fat frame up the hill towards the station refers to herself as an 'hysterical old hag . . . destroyed with sorrow and pining and gentility and churchgoing and fat and rheumatism and childlessness'.[3] She seeks the aid of her fellow-churchgoer Miss Fitt who does not recognise her at first because, though in church they have knelt side by side, in church 'I am alone with my Maker.' When the exhausted Mrs Rooney demands her arm in desperation, her reply – 'resignedly' – is 'Well, I suppose it is the Protestant thing to do.' When they get stuck together toiling up the steps, Mrs Rooney remarks 'Now we are the laughing-stock of the twenty-six counties.'[4] The external references frame Beckett's mocking humour which is also self-parody. And they prepare us comically for the tragedy to come.

The train is late. Mrs Rooney panics because she thinks her blind husband is not on it, and when she finds him being guided along the platform by Jerry the young boy, the comic mood gets darker. Rooney's illness has made their courtship and marriage a disaster. Their married life is childless. Rooney tries to recount as they struggle home in the wind and the rain the reason for the train's long delay out on the line but his blindness prevents him from knowing the location. He agonises over whether the 'hinney' which Christ rode into Jerusalem was barren or procreative. He then discovers from his wife that the text for the new preacher's Sunday service is 'The Lord upholdeth all that fall and raiseth up all those that be bowed down.' The shock ending plays on the ironic juxtaposition of salvation and childlessness, barrenness and procreation. Jerry the boy catches them up in the rain to give back to Rooney an unexplained object he has dropped. At that point, with the final words of the play, he tells Mrs Rooney the reason for the train's delay which her husband had been unable to give her. A little child had fallen out of the carriage, onto the line, and under the wheels.

The Lord has failed to uphold the child that has fallen. The child's tragic death, about which Rooney seems not to have known, though that is ambiguous, echoes the failure of the child they have never had to be born. The couple have ironically missed out on the death of childhood just as they have missed out on its birth. In both cases progeny is destroyed. There is no one to succeed them into the future and no Christian miracle to ensure survival, let alone salvation. It is personal tragedy as well as the Death of God, a combination which suggests, however obliquely, the end of the Anglo-Irish ascendancy. Theirs is a dying race devastated by the tragic accidents their God is powerless or unwilling to prevent. Here Beckett, it should be noted, naturalises the more muted Christian themes of *Godot* and *Endgame*. The play briefly goes against the trend towards greater minimalism and abstraction in the drama after *Happy Days*. It gives us in the struggle home of the Rooneys through the June tempest a naturalised image of the blind Pozzo and the bound Lucky in the second act of *Godot*. The boy, too, with his brief double appearance, repeats the double appearance of the boy in Godot who brings no glad tidings. The question of progeny also echoes Hamm's chronicle in *Endgame* where the child of whom he speaks arriving at the doorstep on Christmas could well be Clov, to whom he has just been speaking. In *All That Fall*, the child who dies and Jerry who brings the news of it are both versions of the child the couple have never had, the child who could continue the line.

All That Fall materialises the vision of the previous plays, albeit through a radio work for voices. It places the themes and shows us why in their particularity of time and place they do and do not work. It is too harsh to see in Beckett's vision of old age the historical redundancy of closet colonials assiduously masked. But the sense is clearly of an historical superfluity made ahistorical and yet also universal. The Irish has become the global and, as if to remind us of it, this play situates the universal impulse back in its particular locale. The world of the French countryside gives way to the world of the Dublin foothills. That use of landmark reminds us that *Godot* with its paucity of reference could be either or both or neither. Yet its topography could indeed be the foreign based on the native, the imprint of uprbinging superimposed on the images of exile. At times the almost bare stage of *Godot* is a blankness which induces double vision.

Yet Beckett's roots go historically deeper. His drama confronts the same crisis of value in European culture as Joyce's fiction and Eliot's poetry. But it does so thirty years on from *The Waste Land*. One sees, as in Eliot or Heidegger, a stifled anguish at the prospect of a desolate world without redemption. If Eliot is minimal and Heidegger abstract, Beckett is both. Yet there is clearly more to his work than this. A cryptic but insistent Christian lineage disting- uishes him from the rational and secular existentialism of the French philosophers. It also means there is no easy comparison between Beckett's plays and those of Jean-Paul Sartre or Albert Camus. Sartre and Camus had both tried to dramatise philosophic- al concepts with mixed success. *Caligula, Requiem for a Nun, Men Without Shadows* and *Altona* all demonstrate the limitations of their approach and in retrospect Brecht, Genet and Beckett have made them seem clumsy and too literary. *Caligula*, which has great clarity and power, is still more of a philosophical rather than a dramatic piece. *Godot* by contrast shows us it is possible to be dramatic and philosophical at the same time.

The startling exception to the general weakness of existential drama is Sartre's *Huis Clos*. But it works because it goes beyond the parameters of secular humanism. With its mocking combination of the natural and the supernatural, the 'hell' that is other people occurs in the eternity of an afterlife. But the space which eternity occupies is that of a French drawing-room, that elegant capsule of naturalism from which there is no exit. This witty supernatural 'play' on the naturalist trap highlights the failure of the existential- ists elsewhere to provide a viable alternative to dramatic realism. *Huis Clos* works as an unusual illustration of a familiar dilemma. Its three protagonists awake to a grim knowledge of each other and

themselves. But it is a knowledge powerless to alter their predicament. They cannot leave each other's presence. The same is true of
Didi and Gogo who are doomed to remain together. Here, however, there is a vital difference. In Beckett, even the basic recognition
that hell is other people goes unrecognised by its sufferers. It can
be clearly seen by Beckett's audience, but their knowledge is a
knowledge which his characters cannot share. It is also appropriate
that Beckett's version of 'no exit', in which Didi and Gogo finally
stay where they are, should occur on an open road where there are
no walls or doors to stop them. In placing them in the open he
simultaneously dramatises and challenges existential conventions.
His play shows equally the power of existential insight and the
limitations of existentialist doctrine.

This of course is not a conscious ploy on Beckett's part. But his
work gains meaning in the context of existentialism just as the
fiction of the nineteenth-century English novelists gained meaning
in the context of the doctrine of progress. As a response to the
devaluation of value and the denial of transcendence, it has
marked a significant break with the previous development of
Western philosophy from Descartes onwards. Its ontology of being
has not only challenged the Cartesian dualism of body and soul
but has tried to locate a place for the authentic self in a starkly
inauthentic world, a nucleus of selfhood in a world without
transcendence. The strongest statement of this has come from
Martin Heidegger. Heidegger has insisted that the solitary person,
confronted by the inauthentic 'they' of the social thrust upon them,
can only resolve the question of their being through the free and
authentic project of a life lived in the expectation of death. For
Heidegger, the primal and joyless modalities of human existence
(*Dasein*) are anxiety, guilt and care. These force one into a resolute-
ness (Heidegger) or an *engagement* (Sartre) in which *Dasein* takes on
its own authentic being.

For Heiddeger the particular being who partakes of authentic
Being in this way becomes an agent of Being's revelation.[5] In this
sense the Cartesian separation of a perceiving subject from a
perceived world is impossible. The particular being becomes the
point of illumination where Being radiates forth. There can be no
absolute separation. With less optimism Sartre argues for a greater
or provisional separation. He sees human consciousness as the
void or nothingness surrounded by objects of Being in the world at
large. But he claims for that very reason the self must be the

foundation of all action and value. In so far as it consciously chooses to act it confronts the very consciousness, its own, which had previously been a void. Sartre's forging of an existential dualism out of the void of self paradoxically gives to selfhood an ontological status which it lacks in Heidegger. He replaces the celebration of the oneness of Being with the self's conscious knowledge of nothingness.

In Beckett's work, neither form of existentialism receives any comfort. For him, nothing radiates forth at the point of Being. There is no radiant light and no revelation. Moreover, the conscious resolution to act cannot conjure the self out of its own void. Didi and Gogo resolve to leave the stage but do not do so. Instead the rhetorical Didi and the hyperactive Gogo are alternative versions of an impossible selfhood. Unlike the incandescent monism of Heidegger's world where the landscape is at one with the horizon, Beckett's world is one where the landscape is unrecognisable and where there is always a further world beyond in the wings and the auditorium. His modes of dramatic being imply not only predicament but also performance, the tortures of endless waiting in which comic play defers the sharing of private nightmares. Like O'Casey, Beckett will often try to laugh away the sting of tragedy, but never completely. For stand-up comedy is but a series of flickering lights in a sea of darkness. At any moment the routines of the music hall can descend without warning into the pitch-black of mortal anguish. Any residual light, any light in the clearing comes only from realising there is no meaning to being at all. The only revelation is that there is no revelation, the only salvation that there is no salvation. Dramatic climaxes repeat themselves and nothing happens. They are profoundly anti-climactic.

Beckett's suppressed Christian genealogy echoes the more explicit pattern of allusions in *The Waste Land*. Myth or no myth, Eliot threads the imagistic path of his 'Son of Man' along the 'wasteland' of post-war Europe whose dry and barren trails recall the desert rock of the Holy Land awaiting its Messiah in a travesty of the Second Coming. Amidst the vacant crowd that surges every morning over Westminster Bridge, amidst the ease of quick sex and torture of long silences, amidst the 'heap of broken images', there is always the trailing echo of the Saviour's force. From 'out of this stony rubbish' grow the fleeting images of the 'third who always walks beside you'. The blank verse reverberates with snatched glimpses of the 'Hanged Man', of Christ crucified but still on earth, an uncanny presence which outlasts the madness of the poem's and the poet's ending. There is in Eliot always the hope of a path back, a path which he takes in his vision of a partially restored pastoral England, in the mystic communion of *Ash Wednesday* and those suberb cadences of *The Four Quartets* which find their way out of urban darkness into a tentative unity with nature, frail in its recurrent uncertainties.

In Beckett there is no path back. *Godot* and *Endgame* are the way forward from *The Waste Land* which Eliot never took, the path that leads nowhere. In *Godot*, Beckett's open road has all the openness of Eliot's barren landscape but Godot never comes. The idea of salvation, sacred or secular, is extinct. Yet Eliot's heap of broken images finds a dramaturgical echo in Beckett's stifled stories, the disremembered parables of crucifixion and salvation that Didi and Gogo blurt out in snatches of unfinished question and answer. Such fractured parables are narratives spurring associations which are never complete, of stories whose endings are never told. The Gospel story of the thieves is the main case in point. Didi who cannot remember it hopes that Gogo will jog his mind into recognition. But Gogo responds blankly, since for him the Bible is an even more distant memory. 'I remember the maps of the Holy Land,' he says. 'Coloured they were. Very pretty. The Dead Sea was pale blue. The very look of it made me thirsty. That's where we'll go, I used to say, that's where we'll go for our honeymoon. We'll swim. We'll be happy.'[6]

The humour lies not only in the quick movement from the sacred to the profane. It lies equally in the blissful forgetting of the original source, the trace of a pleasant memory without its object. That bliss foils Didi's rhetoric of crucifixion. But only for a moment. Didi will set out once more to tell the story of the two thieves he never finishes. It is also the story of Didi and Gogo themselves. This intermittent dabbling with truncated parables is the *oratio obliqua* of self-knowledge. Yet Didi and Gogo talk about themselves without knowing it. Only the audience can know what they strive towards. For they falter without ever reaching their elusive object. Such narrative functions of story-telling have since passed on to Pinter and Shepard. Henry, Lenny, Anna and Deeley, Weston, Eddie and May all tell stories about themselves. Yet Beckett's primal disrecognition is modified by the later playwrights to offset truth against fabrication, deception against self-deception. The characters of Pinter and Shepard talk not in parables but of incidents and histories. They are the explicit subjects of their narrative. Their story-telling externalises the psyche through performance.

In *Godot* and *Endgame*, however, story-telling is at its most integral. In *Godot* much of the tragicomic pathos derives from half-told stories and the interruptions which ensure they never get fully told. By never completing the stories of others, Didi and Gogo ensure the story of themselves will never be told. Hamm, by contrast, ends up as the unchallenged chronicler of a completed story whose meaning he cannot fully recognise. In *Godot* the parallel between the two thieves and Didi and Gogo gradually dawns on the audience. Both are damned by a fate they cannot control and rely on the miracle of a last-minute intervention. In one of the Gospels one of the thieves is saved, but here Godot never comes. The parallel, however, is never a perfect one. The thieves want to be saved from death, and possibly from hell, while Didi and Gogo want to be saved from the boredom of living and discuss the parable to pass the time. The dialogue seems to pass casually and stupidly over the central issues of Christian belief. 'Our what?', Gogo asks when Didi speaks of 'our Saviour'. They establish that one of the thieves is damned and the other saved. At first Didi claims he is saved from 'hell' but when Gogo asks again he exclaims 'Imbecile! From death,'[7] as if he had merely repeated what he had just said. But of course, in the alteration of one word, he changes the theology completely.

The confusion of 'death' and 'hell' in Didi's account is a comic savaging of Christian doctrine and its inconsistencies. To be saved from hell is hardly the same as being saved from crucifixion. The irony is, of course, that Didi and Gogo wished to be saved from neither. They wished to be saved from life. The purgatory of their life offers little hope of salvation except through comic relief. But the humour is evanescent, constantly fading. The horror is turned into a joke which in turn becomes horrifying. For light relief Gogo surveys the audience and comments 'Charming spot . . . Inspiring prospects.' Such distraction from the horror of feeling oneself damned to existence is turned into the farce of forgetting. Neither can decide whether they recognise the place they are in, whether they were there yesterday, what day it is today and what day it was that Godot had asked them to wait for him. Exhausted by such fruitless agitation, Gogo falls asleep only to find that dreaming is an even greater horror. But Didi does not wish to share his private nightmares. 'Let them remain private', he snaps. The denial of

dreaming echoes the denial of salvation and the image of crucifixion soon looms again. They decide to hang themselves from a
tree only to hold back when they cannot do it simultaneously from
the same branch; should one die and the branch break, the other
will be left to endure alone. All that is left is to wait for Godot.

These matching denials of redemption, of dreams and of stories
point to a deeper absence which can only be redeemed by play.
Play is the dreamy surrogate of redemption which arises out of the
denial of redemption and of dreaming. Stories, dreams and the
hope of being saved all threaten to expose an inner world of self
which is so threatening because of its emptiness. But in the public
world also, the two have nothing. Material matches spiritual
destitution. 'We've lost our rights?' Gogo inquires. 'We waived
them', Didi replies. Included as forgotten underlings they are
excluded as destitute nonentities. The structures of feeling working through them are also limits of feeling, ingenious but limited
responses to the world. They are not, in any formal sense,
ideological. They exist beneath formal ideology but also, as dramatic constructs, beyond it. Their stupor and confusion suggest not so
much a false consciousness as no genuine consciousness at all.
Their *ad hoc* play suggests the eternal recurrence of escape from the
disastrous consequences. Nightmares are quickly forgotten when
Didi's turnip turns out to be a carrot and provides a brief
distraction from the passing of time.

Yet Beckett does provide them with a test of their powers of
perception, their capacity for feeling. Without warning he ushers
in an alternative to the barren wayside without rights of possession. It is the world of master and slave. The land which could
belong to anybody appears to belong to Pozzo. The shock of the
spectacle confronting them, the lassoed Lucky trudging in bearing
bag, stool, greatcoat and picnic basket, is a superb dramatic touch.
For desolate equals to recognise dependent hierarchy in such
grotesque form is a test of any on-the-hoof hermeneutics. They are
not equal to the task. Pozzo may recognise them as fellow-humans
of an imperfect likeness. But they cannot recognise Pozzo or Lucky
at all. They might as well be Martians, or Godot and his servant.
Hence the hilarious confusion:[8]

ESTRAGON (*undertone*): Is that him?
VLADIMIR: Godot?
ESTRAGON: Yes.
POZZO: I present myself. Pozzo.

The scene where Pozzo treats Lucky as an animal expected to have the attributes of a servant is like a cruel circus routine. It extends the tragicomic play on the limits of perception. Didi and Gogo peer at Lucky, examine the running sore caused by the rope around his neck, query the bags he never lets drop and are tempted by pity, in spite of their own advanced destitution. The kick on the shins Gogo receives when Lucky weeps but spitefully resists the attempt to wipe away his tears with a handkerchief is a salutary warning. Compassion is not appreciated by those who suffer, only those who put themselves in the place of the victims. The shock of the kick in the shins is a telling blow. Pozzo's ironic coda on the constant quantities of laughter and sadness in the world shows how quickly and effectively he can move from the concrete to the universal. Pozzo claims there is a constant amount of laughter in the world so that if some laugh, others must cease doing so. He then laughs at his own observation. The noise of his mirth is darkly mordant, and after it we can imagine the smiles it wipes from the faces of others.

Beckett twists the knife in even further. Lucky's great outburst into speech reinforces the denial of pity. And the denial of pity confirms the earlier denial of redemption as Beckett stands all Blakean values on their head. The speech is quintessential shock, both in the nature of its delivery and the response it elicits. At one level it is an oblique story revolving around the image of a human skull shrinking and crushed by stones in a world made unbearable by divine apathy. Here it is a fragmented post-Christian parable in the manner of the unfinished story of the two thieves. But the medium is also the message. It is a tale told by an idiot in the high prolix style of professorial gibberish. Didi and Gogo fail to clear their way through the verbiage and hear beyond an echo of their repressed Christian angst. The limits of understanding congeal dramatically into the limits of language. The incessant repetitions of this unending and ungrammatical assault on the ears brings 'protest', 'groaning' and 'general outcry' from an audience of three. Their physical reactions of outrage, which end with all three throwing themselves on the hapless speaker, acts as a visual counterpoint to the deeply buried cadences in the speech. In the confusion it is difficult to tell what bothers the three more, the desolate message or the impossible style of delivery.

As a recitation, the speech is an aborted entertainment, cut short by an enraged audience who feel cheated out of value for money, a reflexive reaction to Beckett's play itself. The 'truth' Lucky speaks is ineffable, not only congealed in impossible language but ensnared by impossible performance. Truth is only revealed by its failure to be revealed. But that is there for the audience to learn. Didi and Gogo learn nothing at all, save that unexpected happenings can always be a source of entertainment. 'That passed the time', Vladimir remarks as Pozzo and Lucky exit. Despite this, the traces of the elusive Saviour remain. Didi, who tried to compare them both to the thieves, is surpassed by Gogo who, abandoning his boots and walking barefoot, compares himself to Christ. But his Christ is the Christ of the quick crucifixion in a warm, dry land. He himself is too old and tired to find the rope that can hang him from the solitary tree.

The second act is a masterpiece of repetition, a triumphant play on sameness and difference. Pozzo and Lucky reappear. Gogo manages once more to mistake Pozzo for Godot. He also tells of another dream Didi refuses to hear. He asks again for a carrot whereupon Didi again brings out a pocketful of turnips. Again Gogo tries on the boots that do not fit him, having found them where he left them. But the differences are as vital. This time Pozzo is blind. This time Lucky is dumb. This time Didi gives his companion a radish instead of a carrot. This time the boy who appears may be the brother of the one who appeared before. The single day which elapses between the acts means that Beckett has moved from a continuous present where nothing in the past was certain to a present bounded by what has previously happened on-stage. In this respect Didi has coherent powers of recall, if an unreliable memory. Gogo has barely any memory at all. The audience can now judge their diminished judgement on the evidence before them. The difference between the two widens as Didi tries to recall a pattern to events and Gogo's memory fails entirely at crucial moments. Gogo cannot remember the tree from the day before, the names of Pozzo and Lucky, the motives of the ten men he claims have beaten him between the acts, or the name of the landscape which surrounds them. 'All my lousy life I've crawled about in mud!' he complains, 'And you talk to me about scenery!'[9]

As it repeats itself, play-acting regresses. But this regress seems more and more to confirm the status of the characters as objects. This objectification is enhanced by the role of Godot himself. The invisibility of Godot, the man, whose name echoes that of God, recalls another god whose nature is strictly material, the God of Capital whose ubiquity Marx analysed with such precise complexity. On one level, Didi and Gogo are poignant parodies of formally free labour, unwitting refugees from feudalism, forced to sell what they do not even realise they own to somebody they have never met and could not even recognise if they did. The macabre joke is that by the end of the play they have failed to sell themselves. They are not even competent enough to reproduce themselves as commodities. Having nothing of substance to alienate, they are not even capable of becoming objects. If we take the term 'employed' as the synonym of labour being useful and being used, Didi and Gogo get around to neither. Their use-value remains untapped, but then they have little use. Denied the privilege of being used, they also realise they are not 'tied' as Lucky is. Here much of the play's suspense comes from them, and us, seeing what they are not, the strange tethered amalgam of serf, retainer, lackey and slave that Lucky has become. As rejects of capital, they witness without recognition the stooping minion who grotesquely encapsulates all of Capital's prehistory.

His servitude is part of a world they do not understand but still fear. They see vaguely the lost humanity of a man turned animal, addressed by his master as a 'pig' and treated like a dog. But their frail compassion cannot hold. Estragon repays the kick on the shin he receives in the first act with a series of kicks to Lucky's prostrate body in the second. At the same time Pozzo's blindness encapsulates the fall of tyrants made helpless by dependence on their victims. Beckett avoids the derision which is a clear temptation after the comic choreography of Pozzo and Lucky's fall. His great power is in refusing to categorise any of his humans as subhumans despite their fallenness, and the compassion his characters lack nonetheless hits the spectator through the anguish of disrecognition. In this way Pozzo, the blinded tyrant who just happens to be an Anglo–Irish landowner, evokes compassion when perhaps he deserves none. His fall is marked in a specific way. He shares with Didi and Gogo the demise of memory and identity. 'I don't remember having met anyone yesterday,' he tells them. 'But tomorrow I won't remember having met anyone today.'[10]

In this strange synthetic fusion of Marx, Freud and Heidegger, Beckett's placing of Didi and Gogo's waiting is one which goes far beyond existential presence. It incorporates the waiting of boredom with the waiting of unvalued labour and the regress of play. The ways of killing time which have made the play so compelling also strike a raw nerve with long-term prisoners in our own culture, as Rick Cluchey's productions have shown. The link with Genet, a real-life prisoner, becomes even clearer. But Beckett's plays go deeper. They make waiting the curse of wanting one's valueless world to be valued, an impossible wish. The final way to kill time is to kill oneself, and hope the gesture of self-crucifixion leads when all else has failed to being redeemed. Of course it does not. But the legacy of Christian yearning goes against the grain of waiting. A stifled Messsianic yearning becomes a futile and incomplete protest against being put permanently 'on hold'. This clash between impulse and predicament is deep-rooted. But it is also unresolved. We know that for all their botched parables, religion is never going to become the opium of Didi and Gogo. At the end, when the last option of hanging themselves with Estragon's belt is rejected, waiting becomes the only possible salvation. They can neither go to their death or move from the stage. The absent Godot is not absent because he has not come, but because he would not be recognised even if he did. And in his absence which can never be turned into presence, the stage is the place where nothing really happens, where performance is the be-all and the end-all of passing the time, of swallowing up the void.

If *Godot's* Irish genealogy recalls *The Well of the Saints*, then *Endgame* comes just as strongly out of Yeats's *Purgatory*. The poet's late verse play is like a flash of lightning, sudden, illuminating and over almost as soon as it has begun. But the movement is perhaps more significant than the movement from Synge. In that case Beckett had extended the tragicomic. In this case the tragicomic takes the place of tragedy. In *Purgatory* an Old Man chronicles the story of his birth to a noble lady and a stable groom. It turns out he has killed his father in revenge and now proceeds to kill with the same jack-knife the very son to whom he has just told the story of his birth outside the ruin of his mother's ancestral home. Before killing the hapless son to whom he explains the genealogy, he sees the purgatorial figure of his mother under a light in the house, a hallucination of her as a young girl awaiting the groom who is to be his father. Like Hamm in *Endgame* the Old Man tyrannises those who come before him and those who come after, tormented by inheritance. *Purgatory* repeats the past through the ritual murder of the son which echoes the ritual murder of the father. But the second murder fails to exorcise the haunting memory of the hoofbeats bringing the groom to his mother, or break the haunting of the house by the dream of his mother's purgatorial soul. The play ends with the Old Man's vain plea to God to appease the misery of the living and the remorse of the dead. The brevity of the play is breathtaking. It seems to contain at source all the anguished play on genealogy which later reverberates through *Endgame*, *The Homecoming*, *Buried Child* and *Fool for Love*.

What Yeats lacks, however, is a form of theatre to realise his rituals and his images. Only the light from the haunted ruin of the house illuminates the darkness of the Boy and the Old Man. Beckett, by contrast, tries to trap genealogy in the enclosed room that could be the inside of a nuclear bunker or equally the inside of a human skull. His room is a mockery of a room with a view. For its 'view' can never properly be described. The exterior darkness of *Purgatory* is replaced here by an unseen greyness. The stage is practically bare but the play still contrives to be about the clutter of objects. Possessing one character who cannot sit down or stand still, it has a petrifying stasis. In *Purgatory* the dead father and purgatorial mother at the window are brief haunting images of the imagination. In *Endgame* the mother and father are dumped in dustbins with closed lids, invisible save for the occasional surge upward, wasting away to death in the presence of their merciless offspring.

The vital shift, tragic to tragicomic, becomes clearer. Yeats's noble Irish ruin is a nostalgic echo of an aristocratic age. But Hamm's stockade is the surviving relic of a perished humanity. What is left is patently ignoble. Compared to Hamm's cruel defensive bluster, Yeatsian parricide seems an honourable though desperate act. Trapped and sedentary, Hamm is a travesty of a tragic monarch, a chess king moving one space at a time in the wrong direction. Stuck in a decrepit sofa with castors that stands in for a movable throne, the blind Hamm who is no Hamlet hams his own nemesis. He is the vestige of a tragic hero, too mean and limited to incite catharsis. Behind his tetchy despair, his author's comic derision looms large. For Beckett, all authority is ignoble and impotent. The play is darker than *Godot*. The compassionate play which binds Didi and Gogo into an intermittent tenderness has no equivalent here. It is a feature of play among equals and here there is none. Even the pity engendered by the fall of the blind Pozzo finds little echo in the seated Hamm. The fitful and painful attempts of Nagg and Nell to make contact are so pitiful they barely connote play at all. If, to invoke Bakhtin and Barthes in a single phrase, Didi and Gogo offer us a dialogic consciousness degree zero, then Hamm and Clov offer us no dialogue at all. Their words are separate, apart. They never flow into each other. And yet as it goes on, their dialogue has all the air of a repartee, an elaborate preconceived game.

When Hamm says right at the beginning, 'Me ... to play', the moves he makes are not part of any recognisable game. They have no apparent structure and little context. Moreover, they seem to have no meaning. His excursions along the chessboard stage are a travesty of the doomed king of Renaissance tragedy resolving, as Richard II does, to defend his kingdom when it is too late. Although it is too late there is little sense of loss, no last defiance. Comically he goes through the motions. His 'moves' are plays with no strategy, his opponents invisible. The 'endgame' is a known routine. It is a move towards closure, but not closure itself. Hamm is playing at apocalypse and if the end does not come we sense that he can play the routine all over again. His waiting for the end and the end itself have no guaranteed convergence. But their possible convergence is what creates the play's dramatic suspense.

This structure without obvious structures is perhaps the hardest image of indeterminacy Beckett has ever mustered. But it is an appropriate image for the century of total war. In an earlier draft of the play Beckett had situated Hamm's shelter in a ruined landscape in France between 1914 and 1918. It is right, however, that finally it has no focus of time or place because it can equally serve as a shelter – and a hopeless one at that – from the threat of nuclear attack. Indeed the latter is perhaps more apt for one good reason – the constant deferring of an attack which could only be final. The 'end' in this sense would signify not merely the end of Hamm and Clov but the end of everything. Yet the deferring through 'deterrence' merely puts off into the near future the likely end that is feared by so many, including Hamm. But while others, presumably, live out their daily lives, Hamm has retreated into the shelter. In that sense he is rehearsing for the end every day in the expectation that one day the rehearsal will become the real thing. Going through the motions of Armageddon, which has not yet come, is still founded on the possibility that it will come, suddenly and without warning. Yet there is no final certainty one way or the other. In the absence of its coming, doom becomes a mere conceit.

As Hamm's servant, Clov is forced to be the servant of that conceit, a dubious mediator between the world outside and his blind master. Never has an unseen exterior of any contemporary play had such a capacity to terrify. Clov's descriptions affect his master just as the description of Burnham Wood moving to Dunsinane terrifies Macbeth. Macduff's army in camouflage provides, however, a naturalistic version of a supernatural prophecy. Its truth is provided by its victorious arrival. Clov has no absolute guarantee from nature or the supernatural. His view from the two high, tiny windows has no prophecy to rely on, or fulfil, no metaphorical language to give it shape. We cannot know what relation his description of the landscape has to a landscape no one else can see. Yet his terrifying descriptions can also amuse. They are part of a comic ritual of satisfying the demands of one's master, as routine as sending messages or preparing high tea, but with no clear means of satisfaction.

If *Godot* is the parable of an absent person, *Endgame* is the parable of an absent world. Here Clov's ways of describing are impacted with disrecognitions. We feel at times that his language cannot match the awesome sight which meets his eyes, at other times that he is trying to say what he imagines his master wants to hear, and yet again at other times we can feel that he is saying precisely what he thinks his master does *not* want to hear. The shock of the description is made more intense by its uncertain nature. It may be there are no words for what he sees. It may be that he recites what his master wishes to hear as part of the routine of apocalypse. It may be that he maliciously deceives the blind tyrant who demands the ritual report upon what he cannot see. There is no clear interpretation. Beckett's professed celebration of ignorance and impotence, of the 'no-knower' finds its true structure here, in performance rather than narration. Yet in his drama there still is a residual narrative. It is performed narrative rather than fictional narrative which gives disrecognition its power. It lies in the tale told to the Other which can be challenged but never falsified, where not only memory but the evidence of the senses fail to guarantee anything.

For Beckett it is the audience who must make the connections. In *All That Fall* the death of Minnie, Maddy's daughter, the 'death' of the little girl under psychoanalysis and the death of the little girl under the wheels of the train must be linked together as broken segments with a deeper theme – the denial of inheritance and, quite possibly, the murder of progeny. In *Endgame* the audience must link Hamm's story about the small boy delivered to his house one Christmas Eve to the presence of Clov. They must also draw their own conclusions. It may be that Hamm is reciting the story of how Clov came to be accepted into the household as an adopted son. It may be that Hamm wills a history of close relationship as a tie that binds them, even if it is not true, even when there are no ties that bind at all. It is ironic that the story is told to his own father now too old and decrepit to recognise a story of paternal compassion. Clov, meanwhile, has left the stage only to return as the story ends. It could well be that he has heard it all before. And it is story more than it is history. 'I'll soon have finished my story', Hamm remarks. 'Unless I bring in other characters.' Then he adds 'But where would I find them?'[11] The ambiguity remains. Has he run out of his powers of invention? Or can he merely fabricate stories about people he knows, those who are in his presence? Can he only tell lies about the living rather than spin tales about the imaginary?

There are no final answers. It is impossible to state categorically that the play is about apocalypse and not the routines of apocalypse, about Armageddon and not the performance of Armageddon. To know one way or the other would be to replace the tragicomic either by melodrama or by mere playfulness. When Clov looks out of the window his failure to find words for what he sees comes as an explosive shock. It may be Beckett's conscious inversion of Genesis with a re-merging of the land and the sea which had once been divided. But more important is the sense that the world Clov sees has gone beyond language. It has become one colour, one shape, one substance. It sounds like the shock of final desolation and yet it may be just a performance which is required of him, with endless patience on behalf of endless repetition, day after day. Though that has a clear comic edge, it is still chilling. The fact of destruction is horrible, but the desire for destruction and, in its absence, for destruction to be performed, is unnerving. The uncertainty as to which it is compounds the unease.

The vision of final desolation is delivered with almost summary dismissal. 'Zero', Clov repeats, 'zero . . . and zero.' The twilight of the day has turned into the twilight of the world. Or has it? When Hamm asks about the waves and then about the sun, 'damn the sun' is Clov's ambiguous reply. When Hamm enquires if it is

already night, Clov looks again through his telescope, then repeats
the word 'grey', getting down from the ladder and finally bellow-
ing the word in Hamm's ear. Hamm's 'Grey! Did I hear you say
grey?' is almost a cue for a blind man's vision of the absence of
colour in the world to be confirmed. Clov's reply 'Light black. From
pole to pole', reinstates the element of darkness.[12] There is a subtle
alternation between the sense of a landscape which is colourless,
and one in which there has been a perceptible darkening. Moreover, we do not know if the 'light dark' Clov sees is the darkness of a
particular night or a permanent predicament. Hamm is kept in
suspense, which is how, perhaps, he wants it to be.

The grey zero Clov fails to describe still evokes a world in which
land and sea have merged. It evokes every cataclysm from the
biblical Flood to the nuclear winter of an unthinkable future. But
there is no objective vision and no sense of place. Hamm's protest
that his servant exaggerates can be played as genuine anxiety or
ritual scepticism. Expecting the shock the decaying tyrant can
dismiss it as a charade. Almost, but never quite. For he can never
be sure, any more than Beckett's audience can be about what lies
outside the two tiny windows. In truth of course nothing lies
outside them except at most a blank backdrop which the stage
directions do not even call for. When Hamm later tells the story of
the mad painter who sees from his window nothing but ashes
instead of the rising corn and the sails of the herring fleet, he is
echoing and demythologising Clov's account of universal greyness. But that account may be precisely what he wants to hear and
Hamm may well be the Emperor without his clothes. The vision of
desolation could exist purely in Clov's imagination or it could be
the malicious lie of a weary servant. But it could also be the
desolate vision of the blind master which the servant routinely
feeds back to him with a sense of duty that has decayed into
cynicism. Whatever the case, each of these different interpretations
leads towards the same conclusion. For Beckett, there is not even
the certainty of recognising final desolation when it comes. The
apocalypse will go unrecognised. It may only be the purgatorial
vision inside a madman's skull or it may be so immense and
horrifying that it cannot be envisaged in advance, no matter how
many times it has been rehearsed. One thing alone is certain.
Humanity cannot go out in that blaze of glory called revelation.

The use of play becomes bolder yet also more problematic in
Krapp's Last Tape. Play becomes a relationship within the split self

between the earlier and the later Krapp, the old man listening to the tape of his middle-aged voice commenting, among other things, on the events of his youth. It is in effect a triangular relationship where the Young Krapp has no presence, the Middle-Aged Krapp is a disembodied voice eloquent but in fragments and the Old Krapp is a decrepit presence with little voice and no eloquence. Disrecognition is equally strong in the reaction of the seventy-nine year old to the thirty-nine year old voice, failing at times to agree, or to understand, or to identify with his earlier self. The play goes against the grain of Proust's 'involuntary memory', the sudden and magic form of redemption by which the past surges into the present through the chance connections of sense-impression. The spool and the recorder are mechanical devices which bring back the past more easily but with little variation. Krapp's dilatory tampering with the machine brings a remembrance of some passages, a complete blankness at others. In Proust the unexpected becomes suddenly familiar. In Beckett the familiar – because mechanically repeated – becomes suddenly disrecognised. The record of what a spool contains in Krapp's ledger can mean at times nothing to him. The word 'viduity' used on tape by the thirty-nine year old sends the seventy-nine year old rushing to the dictionary.

The playing of and with spools is an unreliable play on memory and the past, a playing with former selves, technology made inept. As he switches on and off, changes spools, locks and unlocks drawers, Krapp eats the banana on whose discarded skin he will predictably slip. The 'tape-recording' is an extension of a music-hall routine. But it goes to the limits of the ludic theatre. Play with the Other becomes play with the absent Other, present not so much in spirit as in voice. And the voice of the absent Other is the voice of the forgotten self. As pure voice it is both signifier and signified. It is the raw datum of the thirty-nine year old, the only 'evidence' of that time. Yet the voice is also an unreliable commentary on an even earlier self, a dubious mediator. In all events, play is disembodied and disrecognition becomes both easier and more difficult. The material has been played before to spur some kind of recognition yet the more distant in time the recording becomes, the more its meaning fades from the ageing player of the machine.

The play hangs on one, unique epiphanous moment the Older Krapp will finally refuse to recognise. It is the tape-voice's description of love-making in the drifting punt, unusually ordered and lyrical. It is the voice's supreme moment on that spool and Krapp plays it twice, first as a mere fragment, then extensively. The passion evoked is the play's paradise lost and out of the blue it reinstates the Proustian magic of the remembered instance. But with a vital difference. It has an effect, if at all, on the audience but not on Krapp who can no longer respond to it. Krapp is a man who, Beckett infers, has been fixated on the repetition of favoured moments but in old age can no longer respond to them. The moment moreover is the moment as chronicled, not as remembered. The tape has not recorded the instant of love-making, only the clear epiphanous memory of it. For once the language is precise and radiant. It then offers to the listening Krapp the power of recall he no longer has. But he cannot even recognise what he no longer has. Hence his power of recall has become a commodified object he can no longer consume. If he could, his voice on tape would be emptied of subjectivity even in its most intimate moments. But he refuses to recognise even this. The voice then iterates a moment of lost ecstasy which is as powerful as anything Beckett has ever written. But Beckett, typically severe, disallows empathy. As if to emphasise the infinite regress into which he has been trapped, Krapp is then made to record his comments on the 'stupid bastard' he had taken himself to be thirty years previously. The audience could well deduce that if he lives another ten years and plays this tape back to himself, he could only listen to it with even more stupefying incomprehension, as it contains no evidence as to what it refers. The trap can only be ended now by death.

Along with *Happy Days*, this piece marks the transition from tragicomedy to a minimalist theatre in which the separation of drama from other art forms practically ceases to have meaning. Beckett increasingly interweaves into his dramatic action forms of mime, music, painting, sculpture and poetry which present a total work of art based unusually on a fragment of a text. This astounding and paradoxical relationship between totality and fragment is at its strongest in *Footfalls, Not I, Rockaby* and *Ohio Impromptu*. But it is an abbreviated theatre of stasis and mood, no longer a theatre of play. The powers of innovation are strong but the theatre itself is drastically scaled down and Beckett becomes a miniaturist where thematics of any kind, such as the hysterical recriminations of the love triangle in *Play*, seem to trivialise the purity of the form he seeks. Here it is possible to see in the later plays the forging of a new and minimal *Gesamtkunstwerk* in which movement, gesture, music and words seem formal elements in a constituted whole. Certainly this development has given rise to excited discussion of a 'post-modern' theatre. But if Beckett has moved into new and exciting territory with such a compressed formal purity, he has also had to relinquish the wider dimensions of play.

Such a development was never fortuitous. It was always in the making. The forms of play which nourish tragicomedy are in danger of entropy through constant repetition. The playwright can hint in *Endgame* that the routines of apocalypse will endlessly repeat themselves. To show that endless repetition, however, would lessen the dramatic effect. The effect of such repetition is clear. The more sparing its use, the greater its resonance. But this leads to a paring down and not a broadening, a Calvinist purity which repudiates excess in any form. It leads in the end to a repudiation of play, to a stringent, uncompromising denial. The result is a calculated diminishing. Without play in Beckett, there is no tragic darkness, only darkness itself. The loss of play in his later work is sometimes profound. Yet Beckett had also brought play to its limits. For play itself becomes a trap which finally provides no answers since it merely defers all answering. It remained for Beckett's successors to naturalise play, to take it back into a more recognisable though still disconcerting world. But none could aspire to the blunt paradox of his final achievement. Providing us with a fleeting solution to the death of tragedy, in the next moment Beckett destroys tragedy itself.

Paradoxically, the one later work in which Beckett retains a reflexive conception of play is called *Catastrophe* and is dedicated to Vaclav Havel. Here catastrophe is a measured theatrical effect to be created in a stage rehearsal. But the simulated performance in Beckett's version is pure terror. In the rehearsal the protagonist of the play-within-the play is reduced to an object, dehumanised by the director and his female assistant who put him on a plinth and treat him like a tailor's dummy. He is something to be displayed, something emptied of living, something to be discussed within sight and earshot as if he were a mute victim with no right to reply. The off-stage lighting technician is exhorted to fade up and then fade out the light on the protagonist's body, the moment of 'catastrophe' which will send the director home happy. Yet we experience that beam of light as the final and strongest form of violation against the figure we see on stage. The protagonist then raises his head to acknowledge the audience's distant applause.

The theatre becomes a tight and explosive metaphor of universal terror.

Earlier, Beckett's use of play was a response to a crisis in fiction as much as in drama. Not only did *Endgame* challenge the flickering tragic nobility of *Purgatory*, it also contested the transient compassion of son and surrogate father in *Ulysses*. If Yeats shows the son's murder of the father and the father's murder of the son committed by the same man, Joyce shows the brief fellow-feeling of surrogate father and 'adopted' son, the childless middle-aged Bloom seeking compensation for the early death of his own son, the young Dedalus seeking compensation for the real father whom he derides. In 'Ithaca' one surmises that Bloom and Stephen will never meet again after their nocturnal adventure. The relationship has been fleeting, ghostly, evanescent. The tone is briefly uplifting, quietly affirmative. But little is explicit. *Endgame* inverts this entirely. Clov actively walks out on his surrogate father after a lifetime of intolerable servitude. We see him go. The relationship has been beneficial to neither but the sense of betrayal is not intense enough to issue in tragic and violent death. We sense instead that this too could be part of the performance Clov has given all along and that he could well come back. Beckett is closer here to the supernaturalist trap of *Huis Clos* than to the open structure of Joyce. Neither the tragic minimalism of Yeats nor the comic affirmations of Joyce are adhered to. Beckett's structures of feeling seek an advance and a *via media* in tragicomedy. But they do so at a clear price. One senses that Beckett's dramaturgy leaves him with no exit, with an impossible impasse.

The new structures of feeling he develops in his work show us two vital links between the tragicomic and modernity. The first emerges out of the specific historical conjuncture of Protestant Irish drama and the second out of the general European crisis in modernism. Beckett is at the forefront of the renewed response of modernism to modernity, the return which takes place in the nuclear age. He is one of modernism's great instigators in the period. But his work emerges at a tangent, his drama an oblique translation of a unique Irish sensibility. The Irish play on the English language which he inherited from Joyce and Yeats is at once liberating and rootless. Translated from prose into drama, play becomes a deferring of truth in all its forms, final revelation, final testament, final knowledge. It becomes the freedom of uncertainty combined with the homelessness of exile.

It prompts Beckett to write his plays in French and translate them back into English. This is not of course to be dismissed as a masking, since Beckett's use of the French language is itself extraordinary. But it does bring us back to the disrecognitions in his drama which again have their cultural root in Irish history. Forgetting is both an attribute of modern consciousness locked in the horizons of the present and an attribute of Beckett's Anglo-Irish consciousness, amnesiac in exile. Disrecognition arises out of the Southern passing of Anglo-Irish domination, out of its gradual and imperceptible decay. Like most of the characters in Beckett's plays it is at the end of its life, terminal, finished, but even then uncertain of its state, its quiet agony prolonged beyond obvious cessation. Out of this Beckett forges his dramatic metaphors for the modern predicament. The end of his world, of the world of his family and childhood, becomes in a nuclear age an ominous portent of the end of the whole world. That is why he makes us constantly uneasy, why we secretly wish to dismiss him. It is also why we can never do so.

5

Anglo-Tragic: Pinter and the English Tradition

English tragicomedy was born out of two parallel movements, a native renaissance after Suez and the impact of the modernist renewal taking place elsewhere in Western Europe. It was the age of the loss of Empire. In the theatre it saw a direct challenge to the conventions of the country-house thriller and the drawing-room farce. John Osborne, Arnold Wesker and John Arden all had plays produced by the English Stage Company at the Royal Court which attacked the complacencies of the British Establishment. But it was Harold Pinter who presented the boldest challenge in terms of dramatic form. Without doubt Pinter is indebted to the English naturalism which he acted out in repertory during his early stage career. He makes as much use, even more use, of its possibilities than Osborne or Wesker. Equally he challenges the whole heritage of dramatic realism. In Pinter the Real is always problematic, always in abeyance. He himself has asserted that his stage does not separate truth from falsehood, or appearance from reality. Character, memory, the past, all action off-stage, anything *unseen* can be contested. Pinter distances himself from the earlier tragicomic tradition of Shaw and Chekhov through the legacy of modernist innovation. Here the impact of Joyce, Eliot and Kafka was extremely powerful, while the impact of Beckett was absolute.

Consequently, we have to see Pinter's work in the historical context of the modernist renaissance in English drama. It came about not only during the demise of Empire but during the development of the new consumer capitalism of an electronic age. The work of Pinter, Orton and Bond, all writers who grew up in a working-class environment, confronts that new age and the utopian aspirations which at first surrounded it. Their theatre is one of dislocation, of the lack of connection in the modern city. They go against the grain of the optimisms of the decade, against the liberalist matching of affluence and reason, or the New Left utopia of 'a long revolution', a transformation of working-class life

72

through gradual and enlightened cultural emancipation. The liberal complacencies of assuming greater pleasure and greater choice for all as alternatives to the asceticism and poverty of an earlier period are firmly put in their place in *Saved, Loot* and *The Caretaker*. Williams's vision of an evolving organic community, of a 'long revolution' which articulates authentic voices long repressed by an alien capitalism, finds little comfort here. The closest dramatic parallel to Williams's writing comes in the work of Arnold Wesker, himself a member of the New Left movement of the sixties. But Pinter's work suggests a tragic horror in the daily lives of ordinary people, a wilful and painful evasion of communicating, which renders the early utopias of the New Left shockingly vacuous.

Other playwrights saw things differently to Pinter. In sharp contrast, the political option of Edward Bond for a revolutionary Leninism went largely outside the British theatrical tradition. After *Saved* he tried to develop a form of epic drama to uncover the historical roots of capitalist domination. It was a departure from the study of contemporary working-class life, the choice, as Bond said, of a playwright who was an optimist by nature and a pessimist by experience. The drama of Joe Orton differed for other reasons. It attempted a sacrilegious sexual politics which, like that of Genet, called into question most bourgeois notions of normal sexuality and ridiculed all the ascetic conventions of a pre-consumer society. The idiom of the grotesque farce was the form which, used most effectively in *What the Butler Saw*, allowed Orton to expose the absurdly authoritarian logic of the new welfare state and its divorce from the material needs of its subjects. If Pinter's response was different, however, it was just as important at this point in post-war English society.

Pinter conceived of the life of the city as both a comic and tragic experience. It is hilarious in the failures of its members to define their aspirations and in their compulsive masking of intention, tragic in the victimisation of like by like, in the implosive cruelty of the underprivileged. At times the dividing line between tragic and comic is impossible to make. The city is a drama of the knockabout, of the survival of the fittest. His people are not, however, sentimentalised, mute and suffering, not even the inarticulate Stanley Webber. For Pinter's characters do use language as a weapon in their struggle for survival. They use it not to communicate, not to articulate freely, not to achieve happiness. They use it to dominate others or defend themselves, to evade or ignore. Their use of language, of knowing what to say and when to say it, possesses the native cunning of something deeply embedded in the culture of survival. In the early plays it is a working-class appropriation from middle-class language at times as ingenious as it is economical. But its economy is also a devastating form of self-denial, a willed abnegation. The sentimental notion of a reservoir of noble proletarian feeling which, given the right social conditions, will pour forth as speech and pure expression, finds little encouragement here. The early New Left ideal of articulation as the democratisation of knowledge, of an ideal medium and an ideal language for collective self-expression was simultaneously deconstructed in all of Pinter's early plays. His protagonists are *already* gifted in the use of a diminished language and, existentially speaking, need to be to respond to the unpredictable adversities of the city. But they use language to play games of survival, games in which the power of speech can trap its adherents into positions of weakness from which they can never recover. They are doomed to use the wrong language brilliantly. Their use of that language, however limited and clichéd, is ultimately their own. It is a language appropriated with a view to survival which backfires on its speakers. It becomes their curse and their doom.

In Pinter's later work where he clinically dissects middle-class mores, the use of language subtly alters. There is more control of it as there is a greater rational control by people of their own lives. In *Old Times*, *No Man's Land* and *Betrayal* there is a platform through which his bourgeois characters never fall. They are clearly not victims of their own speech. Language is a refuge from impossible circumstance, not a way of being trapped by it. In his early plays, by contrast, there is a loss of control, a failure to control words in a world of victims victimising each other. This failure often makes us laugh, for it can lead to manic buffoonery. But the utter waste of existence is shattering and there is then a point beyond which, as Pinter pointed out, laughter has to stop. If Beckett takes issue cosmically with the existentialism of the nuclear age, Pinter's work is an antidote to those blueprints of progress which emerged out of post-war England, modest utopias of a rational and sensible future to be had by all. The dystopian decade of the Thatcher government has proved him right. His pessimism should not be seen, however, in terms of a politics of despair. Pinter conveys an abiding sense of human frailty, of the capacity of people to become trapped in their own strategies, to follow the logic of the games they play until it becomes self-defeating. Often the game starts out as the illusion of a playfulness without strings but then turns into a nightmare where all true feeling is suffocated. Performing which starts as a free-for-all quickly turns into the logic of tyranny.

Following Beckett, Pinter pares down the tyranny of performance to an electric tension and a precise detail. But he also moves in a different direction. He provides us with the unseen surrounding of the city. The compression of objects in the claustrophobic spaces of *The Caretaker*, *The Dumb Waiter* and *The Room* suggests the close proximity of a crowded and threatening world. All spaces in which Pinter's protagonists mark out their territory make the rules of the game different from the world outside. The private space is a place of enclosed secrets, almost hermetic. The actions are out of view, out of sight of that unknown world outside the room which the audience finds it difficult to envisage. Just as we cannot know as an audience what is happening outside, no one on the outside, Pinter implies, can know what is happening inside, in the secrecy of the enclosed room. The latter in Pinter is a genuine source of terror, the knife-edge of his black comedy. The world outside, as in *Endgame*, is out of sight but the room inside is also out of sight. In the room inside the fates of Stanley, Gus, Riley and Davies are secretly decided. We share the secret, knowing it to be secret. We are the rapt voyeurs of a threatening secrecy. But the terrorising of victims, which includes in the cases of Gus and Davies the terrorising of terrorisers, is matched by the fearful ignorance the victims have of the world around them. That world is a place of threat whose sting cannot be drawn by Davies's rambling tales or Ben's tabloid anecdotes. For both are tall stories in which the 'outside' cannot be pinned down.

There are two misleading assumptions made in the interpretation of Pinter's work. The first is that an absolute choice has to be made between seeing it as a minefield of Freudian sexuality or as an elaborate set of language-games to which sexuality is irrelevant.[1] It is both and the two are highly compatible. At times they are inseparable. The second mistake is to see his work purely as a modernist inversion of the popular English melodrama, of the country-house thriller or whodunnit whose climaxes consist of a murderer or victim awaiting their fate in a closed room. The dramatic suspense here is one which, as Thompson points out, Pinter had taken over from his acting days in repertory in the fifties.[2] The intruder is the revealed assailant or the triumphant detective inspector, or in some cases one following on the other. This kind of suspense Pinter certainly does use and often with devastating effect. But he does more than make absurd the detective conventions of the three-walled room. For a start many early plays were television or radio plays later adapted for the stage. *The Collection, A Night Out, A Slight Ache, The Lover, Tea Party* and *The Basement* all rely on an open stage or transparent set, or else they use quick scene-changing to break down the scenic fixity of the naturalist room. Pinter's impressive work in the cinema with Joseph Losey also indicates his feel for visual mobility and quick cutting, and feeds back into some of the later plays.

We must consequently set Pinter against his naturalist heritage. His plays are highly mobile, ludic and erotic at the same time. Their subtle variations in dramatic space have an impressive range which has often been ignored. Games of power include sexual games, games which seem to have no rules and no limit but in which, finally, all the players find their moves constrained. The effect is nakedly erotic. This is particularly true of *A Night Out, The Collection* and *The Lover*, but finds its strongest and fullest expression in *The Homecoming*. *The Homecoming* is the most powerful fusion of the two main strands of Pinter's work, the ludic and the erotic, where the playing of sexual games for high stakes has serious consequences. We see here two sides to his drama. The first is the semi-naturalistic, game-playing over territory, over exclusion and inclusion which Pinter sees as a part of working-class city life. This is balanced by a series of 'plays' on the sexual politics of middle-class identity, where exclusion is a feature of an erotic struggle for power that is never finally resolved. In the latter, the more open format of television allows Pinter to use rapid scene-changes and cinematic fades, to break with traditional forms of naturalist partitioning. Where the emphasis is on a fragmented sexual identity as well as the struggle over territory, this is an advantage. Conversely, where the stress is tightly on the invasion of territory, of the private space of others, as in *The Birthday Party* or *The Dumb Waiter*, Pinter retains the tautness of the proscenium stage and the fixed set. The alternatives each have an impressive rationale.

The play which in both these contrasting dimensions are welded most successfully together is *The Homecoming*. The open-plan setting of the room in *The Homecoming* with its added depth of space fuses interior spaciousness with psychic claustrophobia, and opens out the enclosed spaces of the earlier stage plays. Through one family it highlights the conflicting cultures of English middle-class and working-class life. Before it, came the plays of terror originally thought of as plays of menace. The common theme here is the persecution of the outsider, but usually the rationale of persecution is unclear. The identity of real victim is often in doubt until the last minute. The suspense of *The Caretaker* is over Austin's possible exclusion from his brother's home, only for Davies, the intruder, to be shown as more vulnerable. *The Dumb Waiter* has an unnamed victim and two assassins. The final moments of the play reveal to us that one of the assassins is the victim. In *The Birthday Party*, the fate of Stanley Webber is never really in doubt and this tends to make it a weaker dramatic piece. Yet even here the power-play, the conflict over territory and possession, is Pinter's strength. *The Birthday Party* inaugurates many of Pinter's themes, including the dramatic suspense which surrounds the inarticulate victim. But Pinter parodies his victim's persecutors. Goldberg and McCann are deliberate travesties of the music-hall travesties of Jews and Irishmen. Their menace always seems contained by a repartee which never loses its comic rhetoric.

Yet the startling novelty of the play is immediately clear. Through the 'birthday party' that is thrown for Stanley without his consent, Pinter links a regressive and repressive sexuality to an arbitrary and atavistic game-playing. His technique is to offer us the stick and the carrot, terror masquerading as a form of fun. The party takes place only because Meg has interrupted the gruelling interrogation of Stanley by Goldberg and McCann. The sudden switch of direction releases us from the claustrophobia of the interrogation but the sense of menace created by the questioning of Goldberg and McCann is a building-block for what follows. Pinter lightens the mood with the improvised ritual of the party, the game of 'blind-man's buff' which ends in complete black-out. But it is the game, not the questioning, which leads to Stanley's downfall. He displays 'guilt' where none was to be found. In the mêlée of the game, he exorcises his forced Oedipal relationship with his surrogate mother, Meg, by trying to strangle her. He then tries to find his manhood by ravishing Lulu in total darkness. Yet giggling furiously he has also regressed by the end of the game into a kind of childhood in which his desires have a lurid innocence his persecutors interpret as a sign of his guilt. The game becomes evidence of his guilt even though it bears no relation to the things of which he has been accused. Pinter is less interested in the substance of accusation, which seems arbitrary, than the form given it by the power to interrogate and find the crime to fit the accusation.

The party itself suggests a baiting of the victim by allowing him to be the ritual searcher in 'blind-man's buff', of temporarily reversing roles so that his sudden atavism will condemn him to the abduction which has already been planned. For his tormentors the 'crime' has to be created by allowing him to mimic their role. By doing so he seals his own fate. The arbitrary definition of crime is the feature of state terror which finds its most imaginative form in Kafka and the lineage with Kafka is clear. But Pinter cannot find at this point a dramaturgy coherent enough to match the driving force of narrative logic in *The Trial*. Such would be an awesome task and if he fails, it is a brilliant failure. Stanley is too passive for too long, his tormentors too caricatured. But the ingredients of Pinter's work are clearly there, the haplessness of victims and the helplessness of their hopeless friends. Meg and Petey can pretend to themselves that life goes on, that Stanley has still 'to come down' and that nothing has changed. They share a comic but macabre complicity in his abduction.

In *The Hothouse* and *The Room* Pinter continued his experiments in modernist terror, but with varying results. They are perhaps too explicit in their locating of threat, and remind us that Pinter at his best is a formalist who relies on comic effects. *The Hothouse*, a play which Pinter wrote in 1958 but was first staged in 1980, makes too obvious its fable of the abuse of power. By making authority and its trappings so cluttered and so visible it lacks the *frisson* of unseen menace. *The Room* suggests the claustrophobia of *The Dumb Waiter* but relies too much upon its shock ending. Riley, the blind black man who inhabits the basement beneath the room asks Rose, whom he calls 'Sal', to 'come home'. But a different kind of return, Bert's sudden return, costs Riley his life. The play ends melodramatically when Rose stands clutching her eyes, shouting 'I can't see. I can't see.' The play foreshadows, without the humour, many of the qualities of *The Dumb Waiter*. It plays on the threat of exterior space, and in this case, subterranean space, the space below. The dark room of the couple from which they fear to be evicted by their mysterious landlord is heightened by their fear of the even darker basement below, whose darkness finds its nightmarish apotheosis in its black inhabitant. Riley's unexpected plea 'Come home, Sal' thus has an important power to shock, but the frantic action lags without the game-playing of *The Birthday Party* or *The Dumb Waiter* and their comic possibilities.

Of all Pinter's characters, Gus and Ben in *The Dumb Waiter* are the nearest to Didi and Gogo. Uncertainty about their role matches menace with hilarity because it goes beyond caricature. Gus and Ben are more effective than McCann and Goldberg because Pinter dispenses with the excessive rhetoric of interrogation. Instead there is a devastating economy of language as his characters strive to master their bizarre world. The more they try to understand it, the more they become its victims. Having to piece together their part in a killing assignment not unlike previous ones, they dismally fail to do so. They know their elusive boss is called Wilson and Ben, though not Gus, knows they are in a room in Birmingham. Ben claims that Wilson has rented the room for them, Gus that he owns the place, like all the other places in whose rooms they have 'worked'. The room is thus a familiar scene of crime, like all the other rooms with teapots laid on by their invisible boss. But they cannot place it in their world until they start talking about football. Being in Birmingham prompts them to speculate about seeing the Villa play football the following day. But they cannot even work out whether Villa are playing at home or away. The assassins are thus victims of their lack of knowledge. Knowledge is replaced by tabloid sensations as Ben reads out lurid headlines in their newspaper. The action they undertake itself comes to have the feel of a tabloid headline. They thus become commodities, objects for sensational consumption in which the boundaries of fantasy and reality break down.

The power to take life fails to endow them with the dramatic power of tragic figures or even the melodramatic power of sadistic villains. Creating characters whose decisions are already decided for them, Pinter uses their uncertainty as a source of comic pathos. The device of the 'dumb waiter' is at the centre of this masterful strategy. They are on the receiving end of absurd commands, restaurant orders for a restaurant long defunct. Playing a game over which they have no control they have lost before they have started. Here Pinter manages to generate brilliant tension out of the way in which they lose. It is as if their unseen boss can second-guess their uncertainty, as if he has already come between them by gaining the confidence of Ben and playing the game of divide-and-rule. Moreover, it is as if the very *timing* of his inverventions is uncannily exact, probing them at the point of weakness, needling them at the point of exhaustion. The envelope full of matches which slides mysteriously under the door leads to their futile argument over lighting the kettle, only to find that the gas has run out. The first crash of the dumb waiter in the shaft with its first lunch order comes just after they have failed to establish what role they are playing in the mysterious organisation to which they belong. The hilarious response of the two to the increasingly exotic menus they have to make up is also a token of their loss of power for which their revolvers cannot compensate. The killers are fall-guys who matter nothing. The dumb waiter is a superb metonymic symbol of their helplessness. It descends and rises when it wishes to and they become its frantic slaves. It moves between a room that is no longer a restaurant and a basement which is no longer a kitchen.

The invisible game in Pinter is linked to this invisible outside. Taken together they are the key to dramatic space, to the comic terror it generates. Soon after they first enter the room, the foreboding of Gus frames the room as a source of interior darkness 'I wouldn't mind if you had a window, you could see what it looked like outside.'[3] But there is no window and no view. The job takes place in darkness, out of sight, a form of secret terror. Gus and Ben are terrorists without a cause in a room without a view. Wilson, their boss, is a more contemporary version of Godot. In the past he has appeared intermittently but now makes no appearance at all. 'He might come. He might just send a message. He doesn't always come.'[4] Wilson plays a game which degrades them, turning the weapon he masterminds against the terrorists they employ. The play is a constant reminder that in terrorism the terrorist can often become the victim of his own methods. The ghostly menu which keeps changing is a fateful sign of their vulnerability and the dumb waiter's acquisition of their paltry rations becomes a superb comedy of terror. Without the crisps, tea, biscuits and Eccles cake they have just dispatched, they suddenly possess all the transparent weakness of victims. The order for scampi is the straw which breaks the camel's back. Hence Ben's funny but despairing shriek up the tube: 'WE'VE GOT NOTHING LEFT! NOTHING! DO YOU UNDERSTAND?'[5]

This is Pinter at his best. The box in the shaft comes down from the invisible outside and emphasises again the trap of the three-walled room. If Hedda Gabler is powerless to orchestrate events which take place beyond the confines of that room, she can at least gain some report of what has happened. But Gus and Ben simply have no clue as to what is going on. The boss is like the unseen director of the play itself orchestrating the final encounter on-stage where Gus will rush back into the room, stripped of jacket, waistcoat, tie, holster and revolver and present himself unwittingly as the victim. While the hapless pair cannot see beyond the room which has no windows, Wilson appears to have X-ray eyes, tracking their every movement through brick walls, appearing to possess an omniscient and unseen gaze. The proximity of his brooding unseen presence contrasts starkly with the void of the absent Godot. The pair thus pay the price of terrorist secrecy and become its victims. Its implosive power separates out the assassin from his accomplice. One remains the terrorist, the other becomes the victim. This is terrorism without spectacle, its seedy under-belly, its slapstick combination of fear and farce.

The play follows the example of *The Birthday Party*. Circumstance and motive are minimal. Terror and the resistance to terror come through the ritual menace of play, where the ritual is invented by the persecutors. The dumb waiter is a metonym for unanticipated terror. It represents our fear of unpredictable terror by presenting it on-stage as a mute object terrorising living beings. While the goal of terror is serious its means are hilarious. It is a superb example of ludism in which extreme formalism is balanced by existential play. By contrast, the interrogation in *One for the Road* shows Pinter's formalism running into difficulties when it gives up humour because of the thematic seriousness of its topic. The playfulness of the unrelenting and sadistic interrogator is too one-sided. There is no dialogic relationship of victim and victimiser as in Christopher Hampton's *Savages*. The form of the play is narrowly naturalistic, the victims so far abused that they are by now mute and unresist-ing. With the tongue of the father already cut out, terror is reduced to the terrorist's power of speech in the certainty of the victim's silence.

Clearly influenced by *Catastrophe*, Pinter wanted to politicise Beckett's vision, to take the victim off a plinth on a stage and place him on a chair in a police cell. But lacking the ludic power of his earlier plays, *One for the Road* becomes leaden and oppressive in its pessimism. Pinter wants to take us straight into that harrowing moment when the resistance of the just has been broken by agents of state terror. The victims are respectable, not a terrorist cell, but a decent bourgeois family, a nuclear family being denuclearised. The investigator's line in sexual terror is to insinuate the impotence of the mute husband, the taking out of the tongue a symbolic castration as well as a physical maiming. Then he works by innuendo to turn the faithful wife into a common whore. Here terror's power is to turn the person into a fantasised role where the word of terror defines the reality of its victims. The role transformations are powerful, but Pinter omits to name time and place, to take his naturalism through to expected conclusions. His characters, with no farce to diminish them, demand a full identity which the playwright fails to give them. They exist in a limbo. As in the recent *Mountain Language* they are mere ciphers. The play moves in the direction of sympathy but cannot make the final step. There is a danger that because his victims are so passive, the audience will share the interrogator's contempt. By contrast, *The Dumb Waiter* is prophetic, conveying the hazards of the secrecy of terrorism in the contemporary world, a terrorism which suffocates in the insane logic of its claustrophobic necessity. The dialogue has strong echoes of an earlier modernist language. It is indebted to Hemingway's *The Killers* while Gus and Ben, as well as obvious heirs of Didi and Gogo, are also descendants of Doris and Bertha, the bemused prostitutes in Eliot's *Sweeney Agonistes*. The ear for the nuances of class language is undiminished. It constantly echoes the contrast in the second section of the *The Waste Land* between the working-class women in the pub and the middle-class couple who can no longer speak to one another except in fragments. And this division is also another kind of division which he uses constantly, the division between speech and silence.

Pinter's vision of working-class existence in the city is most strongly focused in *The Caretaker*. The play treads a middle path between the moral agonising of Arnold Wesker's trilogy and the bleak, fragmented cruelties of Edward Bond's *Saved*. Pinter does not concern himself with political ideals but with territory and possession, power and exclusion. His view of working-class life is as bleak and uncompromising as Bond's but he still detects within it, in the relationship of the two brothers Mick and Aston, a bedrock of loyalty which cannot be broken. Here, though, all his characters are still diminished by context and circumstance. In the working-class domains of the city, conscience seems not only a luxury but a form of madness. The play on exclusion here is fundamental to Pinter's tragicomedy. The figure of Davies, the vagrant, is set up as a typical eyesore for the settled citizenry of the metropolis. A tramp, a drifter, an opportunist who takes what he can get from the more settled and the more fortunate, he exemplifies a permanent scandal of city life with which people learn to live. As an outsider, the open and exposed character of Davies's wanderings are a known factor. The secret scandal the flat conceals is that of Aston, the insider hidden from public view and protected by his brother, a chilling version of the idiot in the family. The open eyesore of the drifter is matched by the living skeleton in the family cupboard.

The change from Beckett is illuminating. The identity and pairing in *Godot* is split. Davies is a version of Didi and Gogo but so, together, are Mick and Aston. For both brothers Davies is a potential double, the violent and unpredictable barbarian that is Mick, the suitable case for treatment that is Aston. But both brothers reject him. Hoping to find his way into the city in which he is an outsider, hoping that by taking up the offer of a job as caretaker he will take over the residence by stealth, the eccentric parasite hopes to displace the concealed madman. But he is finally shunned and left, at the end, with no option but to leave. His greatest difficulty is to find out the relationship between the two brothers. Seldom together, seldom communicating, they exclude him without appearing to, with no obvious conspiracy. We do not know, any more than Davies does, how they talk to each other, or what secret signs pass between them. He is finally helpless because he cannot undo what he cannot see and does not know.

Set in the cluttered upper-storey room of a West London flat the spatial defence of territory has both an internal and an external dimension. In the verbal struggle for power, Davies projects himself as a peripatetic wanderer who circles the capital's periphery while Mick casually displays to the visitor his insider's knowledge of North London. The expert of the metropolitan bus routes flaunts his expertise at the hobo who has shambled from Luton through Watford, Wembley and Hendon in order, so he claims, to reclaim his papers in Sidcup. Metonymically Mick defends Aston's flat, which he owns, from the threat of the outsider. Rhetorically he defends the inner city from the concentric ramblings of Davies around the North Circular and Western Approach roads. At the core of metonym and rhetoric is the frail brain-damaged brother, the human nucleus of authentic London. And Aston, as we know, is clearly not all there.

The physical dimensions of the play are among the most impressive in Pinter's work. In the cluttered room where objects often have no apparent function, he finds a perfect contrast to the open-space paralysis of Didi and Gogo. Aston's quest to build a shed to give himself more room and more order is self-defeating as he accumulates materials which constrict him even more. The shed is the hidden utopia of dramatic space. In the room itself lies all the junk the shed should contain, the paint-buckets and coal-bucket, the step-ladder and toolboxes, the lawnmower and shopping trolley. The space is a dystopian clutter, gathering objects not for their usefulness but for the opposite reason, their lack of use. Davies wakes to find himself practically with his head in the gas oven, but the oven does not work. Pinter thus reduces staple forms of naturalist scenery, furniture, ornament and appliance to a clutter of impossible junk, as menacing for what it does not do as for what it does.

The other dimension of physicality lies in the relationships between the characters. The play works through physical containment. Mere threat is sufficient if the context is right. At the end of the first act, Mick pushes Davies to the floor and fixes him in a half-nelson. He casually stands on the tramp with his foot as Davies tries vainly to escape. Force here invokes the threat of even greater force. But it gains further strength through rhetorical speech. Playing on his superior strength Mick rhetorically asks his victim 'What's your game?' while sadistically playing games himself. When he wants Davies to leave for good, he shows him the fate of any resistance by smashing the tiny Buddha statue to pieces against the stove. Davies well knows that could be his own fate. Yet the physical will-to-power is inseparable from the verbal will-to-power. Just before smashing the statue Mick pre-empts moral indignation by accusing Davies of vices which easily describe himself: 'Most of what you say is lies. You're violent, you're erratic, you're just completely unpredictable. You're nothing else but a wild animal, when you come down to it. You're a barbarian.'[6]

At times the piece is overwritten. Pinter often loses the economy of language which makes *The Dumb Waiter* so precise. There is too much rhetoric in monologue. The tramp's repeated claim that his papers are in Sidcup is too much of a comedian's catch-phrase while Mick's repertory of casual lies is equally a transparent music-hall device. Mick's challenge which begins 'You remind me of my uncle's brother', and ends 'Your spitting image he was.

Married a Chinaman and went to Jamaica', is too forced to be a credible lie and too funny to constitute a serious threat. The surplus of rhetoric often goes hand in hand with a surplus of obvious falsehood. The tall story is substituted for the Beckettian chronicle. Yet Mick's blunt comic patter is offensive and cumulative. It serves to disarm the audience when Pinter switches to the darker side of experience, when Aston's monologue suggests a tragic dimension to the life that Davies and Mick present as knock-about and picaresque. The comic sets us up for the tragic. Rhetorical surplus which denotes little *per se* generates a mood and a rhythm against which a deeper pathos can assert itself.

Pinter's doubling of Davies and Aston, outsider and insider, at this point becomes devastating. Aston is one of the most powerful and enigmatic of Pinter's creations. He can remind at times of the Russian tradition of the 'holy fool' but equally of those dramatic vessels of poisoned idealism, Gregers Werle in *The Wild Duck* and Hickey, the hardware salesman of *The Iceman Cometh*. But the poison is never apparent. Aston appears after his horrifying confession of electric shock treatment to be the brain-damaged soul of modern working-class London. Yet Pinter is not concerned to model psychic suffering on Dickensian sentimentality. Aston is a victim, certainly, but not a passive victim. Pinter leaves us with a frightening ambiguity. We cannot tell whether Aston's goodness is a residual innocence that hospitalisation has failed to destroy, or whether it is simply a result of that treatment which has damaged him for life, an idiocy of goodness that has little moral meaning. The ambiguity is compounded by the way in which Aston acts. He acts to 'save' Davies, to prevent him getting beaten up in a café and to bring him home for comfort and shelter. He thus seems a naive, at times touching 'good samaritan' living out his life in a daily chaos he is powerless to alter.

Like Werle and Hickey, however, we sense that with Aston to save is also to destroy. His attempt to redeem Davies is an attempt to redeem a brother-in-arms, an outcast like himself who is not, however, on the inside but on the outside. Aston dimly recognises Davies as an estranged version of diminished self, of self-dereliction. But while Davies ungratefully tries to probe the weakness of the 'nutty' elder brother to curry favour with the aggressive younger one, Aston has his own cryptic strategies to match the blatant manipulations of his guest. It is as if his attempt to save Davies is also an attempt to hospitalise him, to echo in his treatment of his alter ego the treatment which has already been afforded him by the state. Certainly we cannot place Aston in the way we are invited to place Davies with his comic non-sequiturs and self-contradictions. At best it seems that Aston wants to save and punish a kindred soul, and that good and evil both work through in ways he cannot understand. Goodness is the desire not to see his experience of suffering repeated in others. Evil is the desire to see that it is. In his damaged persona, both coexist. And both are social constructs. The desire to do good is a social extension of the desire for self-preservation. The desire to commit evil emerges from the vicious circle of a revenge culture in which the memory of personal pain can only be exorcised by witnessing its effect in others.

Aston is the victim who seems to act without malicious intent while the central power struggle appears to exist in the contest between Mick and Davies for Aston's loyalty. A stronger reading of the play, however, comes from seeing Mick and Aston as terrorising Davies through alternate means, one through sarcasm and aggression, the other through attention and compassion. Aston's revenge is to 'care' for his double in the way that he says he has been 'cared' for himself. Just as Gus is a terrorist who eventually becomes a victim, Aston is a victim who eventually becomes a terrorist. The gas stove which does not work but whose taps Davies is scared of knocking on in his sleep, the open window which gives him a constant draught while sleeping, the sleep 'starvation' caused by Aston's rude awakenings are trivial versions of the terror Aston himself claims to have suffered in the asylum. But they blend with the more obvious game of terror which Mick is playing, moving from threat to promise and back more to threat again. Thus the alternate games of terror – Mick's terror as naked threat, Aston's terror as muddled compassion – act like a pincer movement to exclude the outcast who entertains illusions of inclusion as a caretaker. Hence the superb dramatic irony of Aston's version of what a 'care-taker' actually is.

Aston is thus like a child resembling a doll who is playing with a doll, playing at the role of parent yet stranded between affection and abuse. It is the innocent performance of terror through imitation by terror's victim, the guinea-pig of the asylum going through the motions of surveillance over his victim/guest in a room full of junk that can never be a home. As the victim of that terror plus the more explicit terror of his brother, Davies himself is no innocent victim, but rather a guilty one. Victim of a system which gives him one name and tempts him to use another, he combats injustice with inertia and self-righteousness. He in turn is guilty of the contempt of other victims of the system, of women, starting with his discarded wife, of Blacks, Poles and Jews whom he hates with a relentless paranoia. Pinter has called the theme of the play 'love'. But if anything it is about the extirpation of evil by evil. There is no beginning or end to evil, either as an individual propensity or as a social construct. In truth, the two cannot finally be distinguished. Evil, both social and personal, becomes a set of infinitely reflecting mirrors. Mick and Davies mirror each other in the rhetoric of abuse, Aston and Davies in the rhetoric of victimisation, Mick and Aston in the secret bond of terror, without obvious collusion, against the outsider become intruder.

The element of play is understated but reverberates throughout the dramatic action. Its superb moment is the bag-passing scene in which Aston has retrieved Davies's bag only for Mick to snatch it away. It is the one major scene in which Mick and Aston are together but barely a word passes between them. As the bag whizzes back and forth grabbed by Mick, retrieved by Aston, given to Davies, Pinter suddenly changes the order, like pass-the-parcel in reverse. Aston finally imposes his will by giving the bag back to Mick, not to Davies and forcing Mick to give it to the tramp. The action is a comic tour de force. But it is also a reminder of Aston's compassionate game-playing. This in turn should remind us that not even his account of his madness can be taken completely for granted. As we go deeper into the play we are invited tantalisingly to speculate on how far his memory is accurate, how far his madness is real and how far it is performed. We are given no clear answer.

Yet in terms of certainty the play progresses beyond the nightmare fables of *The Birthday Party* and *The Dumb Waiter*. It locates its characters. It naturalises nightmare. Aston and Davies both live out an enduring horror by masking and distorting it, ignoring and exaggerating it. If nothing is absolutely certain, nothing can be absolutely concealed. *The Homecoming* takes this one stage further. It dissects the horror of normality without resorting to extremes. There are no wandering vagrants who fail to make sense of their lives. There are no memories of shock-treatment, real or imagined. Of course, there remains the unreliable chronicle, but this serves to horrify in a matter-of-fact way. Here Pinter's work takes a new turn. What interests him now is the violation of normality by those who are normal.

6
Pinter: The Game of the Shared Experience

The terror of the normal is widely seen as the key to Pinter's modernist powers of invention. The other feature crucial to his tragicomedy but more often ignored is its vast seamless play on sexual sharing. In his diaries Joe Orton claimed that the sexual sharing in *The Homecoming* was inspired by *Entertaining Mr Sloane* but that its explicit use was inappropriate for someone whose personal life was as orthodox as Pinter's.[1] To suggest experience as a necessary basis for drama was, of course, part of Orton's promiscuous bravado. But it is misleading here on two obvious counts. There is no proof that 'experience' in Orton's positivistic sense explains anything. Moreover, the theme of sharing begins in Pinter's work well before *Entertaining Mr Sloane*. It starts with the 'sharing' of Lulu in *The Birthday Party*, and continues with the 'sharing' of Stella in *The Collection* and the 'sharing' of James Fox by Dirk Bogarde and Sarah Miles in Losey's *The Servant*. It takes more oblique forms in *A Night Out* where the hero is shared in spirit though not in flesh by mother and prostitute, while in *The Lover* each of the two spouses is shared between the other and the other's lusting *alter ego* suitably dressed for the occasion. In this world of split identities, Freud's bisexual maxim that in any sex act four people are involved is contained by Pinter with superb dramatic tightness in a heterosexual frame.

If marriage and adultery allow *The Lover* to create a perfect quartet out of two people, it is important also to recognise elsewhere the bisexual dimension of Pinter's sharing. The sharing of the other with the other is a gloss on the same and the different. In *Betrayal* the dramatic force of the husband's recognition that he has been sharing his wife with his best friend propels the audience forward into the meaning of 'best friendship'. Betrayal is thus a two-edged sword. If Emma has betrayed Robert with Jerry, then Jerry has betrayed Robert through her. The oblique sharing in *The Servant* glosses the shifting active and passive conceptions of the transitive verb. If the master shares the servant's fiancée/sister with his servant then the master is finally shared by the servant and his 'sister'. In *The Collection* the pairing of Bill with Harry and James with Stella gives the play an asymmetrical symmetry of same-sex versus heterosexual partners where the latter relationship as a marriage is obviously explicit and the former partly veiled. The explicit crossover effect is the accusation by the husband of adultery by the junior male, Bill, with his wife. The implicit one is the possible relationship which may develop between cuckold and lover whose game-playing duels themselves have an erotic under-tow. As always with Pinter, everything is insinuated yet nothing is certain.

Here sharing is also struggle, both feature and consequence of the will-to-power. But the will-to-power in Pinter is simultaneously linguistic and physical. The body can never triumph without the spoken word while the spoken word, without the potential power of the body, is sterile. The struggle for the object of desire is always matched by the verbal struggle for the accepted version of the truth. In *Old Times* the two are practically inseparable. Deeley and Anna both try to impose their version of the past upon their relationship with Kate, the mute present object of their struggle for possession. In *No Man's Land* Spooner's attempt to ingratiate himself with Hirst in a homosexual household that is hostile to him involves competing through boasting chronicles about past succes-ses with women, including Hirst's former wife. These polysemic memory-games, mysogynist yet heterosexual, are a key to power in the present, homoerotic and potentially violent. The 'memories' of women become weapons in man's struggle for domination over man. The dramatic interplay of speech and act, language and the body, entails a crossing of sexual boundaries which challenges the convention of any sexual boundary.

In *The Collection* Pinter's use of dramatic space highlights the asymmetrical symmetry of the play's sexual boundaries. Adjacent see-through sets of the male couple's Belgravia town-house with period decor and the married couple's Chelsea flat with contem-porary furnishing intimate an incestuous propinquity. Both pairs, it turns out, are boutique-owners and dress-designers. Yet there is also a sense of eerie dislocation. The author's directions – for what initially was a television play – divide the stage into three areas, 'two peninsulas and a promontory', the latter, upstage, centre, being the phone box from which anonymous calls connect the two

parted households. The sense of threat in the telephone voice is
connected not only to James's accusation about his wife when he
appears in the male household, but something deeper. In Pinter, as
in Ibsen, there is always a subtext which runs in counterpoint to
literal meaning. If James accuses Bill, he also pursues him. The
pursuit that is part of the accusation, and threatens to become
violent, can also be seen as a revenge pursuit of desire, the mimicry
of Bill's desire yet more violent, in which James threatens to turn
Bill into the same kind of object which he accuses him of having
made his wife. Making the maker, seducing the seducer is the
latent threat in his aggression as he stands arrogantly at one point
over his fallen victim. Yet we cannot even tell whether the original
seduction actually took place. The 'seduction' of the spouse could
be the pretext as much the context for the seduction of the
'seducer'. Equally the threat of seducing the seducer may just be
part of the strategy of revenge which is never intended to material-
ise, a bluff which is never meant to be called.

Dramatically, the conceit works because the seducer is himself
gay, the kept 'wife' of an older man, alleged to have transgressed
the boundaries of sexual identity by seducing a real wife of the
opposite sex. The knowledge which Pinter succinctly imparts to
the audience of Bill's domestic servitude and of the jealous
possessiveness of Harry, his lover, makes the unspoken strategy of
James more and not less convincing. It also justifies the symmetry
of the reverse anonymous phone call by Harry to Stella, echoing
that of James to Bill. When Harry returns and overhears the
threatening banter of his lover and his lover's accuser, his intervention fuses text and subtext. He intervenes to prevent the situation
getting out of hand after James has carried his duelling game too
far by hurling a knife at Bill's face. But he also intervenes to rescue
his 'wife' from the threat of sexual possession as well as further
physical injury.

Pinter shows himself here to be the master of dramatic intervention with the timing of Harry's return. Harry can play down the
incident of the knife by casually mentioning his congenial visit to
the intruder's wife. He also lies, as the audience sees, about their
conversation. While Stella confides to Harry that she barely saw
Bill during the whole period of their stay in the same Leeds hotel,
and that her husband has simply jumped to the wrong conclusion,
Harry claims to James his wife has admitted making the whole
thing up, that is, admitted accusing Bill of a seduction which never

took place. At one level it is a sign to James to lay off his 'wife' by withdrawing the threat of injury. At another level it is a sign not to lay his 'wife' since he, Harry, who has just chatted to James's wife in James's flat, can reply in kind. It is a perfect stand-off. If James threatens to proceed, then Harry, too, will proceed. The threat is of course an attempt to return to the status quo ante, even though nothing may have happened. For the crossing of boundaries, in the past from gay to straight, in the future, possibly from straight to gay, is not to be permitted. If one 'wife' has seduced another, then the threat of the cuckolded husband raping his wife's seducer must be answered by the seducer's lover also threatening to seduce the wife.

As subtext, the sexual discourse is prevented from serving as a facile and explicit explanation. It is the undertow to the official discourse of the jealous husband and his rage. That of course is assuaged by Harry's judicious intervention. But there is another angle also to that. He tells James, as he has told Stella, that Bill is a 'slum boy' who 'confirms stupid sordid little stories', an upstart lacking, by implication, a certain middle-class finesse.[2] The pejorative repetition of slum adjectivally – 'slum boy', 'slum sense', 'slum mind' and 'slum slug' – in Harry's insulting diatribe points to the hidden motive. The connotation of slum-boy and bum-boy – with 'slum slug' onomatopoetically suggesting 'bum' and 'bug' – immediately comes to mind. The linking of class and sexual power, even in a gay context, is an appeal to the restoring of accepted conventions. The dominant partner in each pair can accept clearly drawn lines of trespass. But the implicit deal has a sting in its tail. Pinter is glossing hypocritical reverence of the bourgeois wife as sacrosanct through the verbal pillory of a slum wife who is neither married nor a woman.

We have here a sense of containment, of the preserving of order which is unspoken but vital. But the containing of order works through the repressing of feeling. Here feeling is both emotion and action. It is the emotional response towards whatever action might have taken place and what action in turn might be provoked. But such re-action must be contained, and the drive toward it curtailed. That sense of curtailment, when the incident with the knife ends dramatically on a note of false *bonhomie*, is echoed in the final version of the meeting in the hotel. It differs from all of the previous versions, which in turn differ from each other. 'You just talked about it, in the lounge' James suggests to Stella, a version she will neither confirm nor deny.[3] The truth is as elusive as the truth of the world outside Hamm's room in *Endgame*. But just talking about it suggests the right sense of distance from the act, for 'just talking' is something that can be contained. It is a form of partial expression, of desire as speech but not yet action, action not yet realised and therefore manageable, nipped in the bud. It also legitimates the sexual status quo, where acceptable transgression would be the conversion of the thought into the spoken word but not into the deed.

It is the bourgeois stand-off which recognises marriage and 'marriage', the coexistence of couples as social doubles, as dress-designers who never can assume a full sexual likeness since one couple remains straight, the other gay. From either side any crossover is a threat. But it can only be a threat if it is already a temptation. The moment in the play when James and Bill stand side by side in front of a mirror looking at their adjacent images visually illustrates both threat and temptation. But the middle-class control of its emancipated sexuality cancels out both by eventually refusing transgression the status of an event. If nothing is to happen in the future then nothing can have 'happened' in the past. Pinter's stage with its two peninsulas and a promontory, the separate and distinct homes that are so near and yet so far, divided by the phone box which is the source of rumour and threat, is a perfect complement to the conceit of contained sexual play in which no one is fully truthful. Here conceit is deceit. No one tells the truth. Dramatised here in miniature as a studio piece, bourgeois society is, as Nietzsche had prophesied, lived out as a lie.

We can see how Pinter gives us a dramatic resolution, a *modernist* resolution of the Freudian problematic posed by *Strange Interlude*. If bourgeois social order is to be maintained then its sexuality must be contained. Contained but not repressed. Instead of O'Neill's thoughtspeech where truths which cannot be spoken to other characters are revealed to the audience, Pinter's truths remain withheld, oblique, a spider's web of possibilities. Intimacy is the central region in which the unspoken truth occurs. Just as lovers intimate their actions only to those who are present, that is themselves, so both audience and outsiders are excluded. Pinter's writing thus gives us the play of exclusion which makes truth so elusive to all, where no couple will ever fully know what one of them has done in conjunction with someone else. Neither will the audience. In *The Collection* the parallel cross-cutting between the two homes, where one lights up on stage as the other is faded out, reinforces the sense of our absent knowledge, the crucial gaps which occur without continuous presence. In this way tragi-comedy becomes the drama of imperfect knowledge. Yet following on from Beckett and Genet, Pinter has also naturalised imperfect knowledge. It no longer inhabits a nowhere land or a house of illusions. It is near at hand, making recognisable landmarks places of the uncanny, abodes of disrecognition.

In *The Lover*, middle-class containment is given a suburban location. The novelty of Pinter's plot is to turn adultery back upon itself, so that spouses enact the role of the Other in which they betray their formal allegiance. The play concerns the betrayal of themselves by themselves. It has a sense of entrapment which builds on naturalist closure, the suburban home as the prison of the middle-class housewife. But the home is also the source of secret intimacy, the inner sanctuary in which everything is permitted by default. Pinter plays here on the paradox of closed prison and secret desire. In doing so he clinically dissects the limits of the truncated self which finds its otherness in fantasy close to home. Home is the source of devotion but only because it is the shrine of lust. The split selves of the suburban couple, husband and lover, wife and mistress intersect through transferred images. The wife meets her 'lover'. Her husband encounters his 'whore'. Ecstasy is experienced through the fantasy of the Other, which is in reality a shrinking from the other, a containment of the other in the split self. Yet such a containment has its price. It can only work as a game in which the adulterers share the secret knowledge of the inadequate spouse who has dissatisfied the married transgressor. In mocking the absent other, however, the real pain of betrayal is exposed. For the other is always present, pretending in their mutual fantasy that he or she isn't, but still hearing the words that injure, the secret words of defamation not meant for their ears.

The defamation of the absent other who is nonetheless present is also part of the battle for power. Richard the husband who returns to his wife as Max calls her Sarah in the morning and Dolores or Mary in the afternoon. Richard/Max and Sarah/Dolores/Mary are perfectly monogamous but remain so only by swapping partners and identities at the same time. Their struggle for power as equals in the conspiracy of transfer revolves around two things, the initial advantage of the transgressing male and the power to wound in the defamation of the absent other. While the wife calls her 'lover' a lover, the husband calls his 'mistress' a whore, echoing the sexual double-standard of adultery which inheres in their class culture. The power to wound is measured, as in much of Pinter, by the success of the partner who flinches less, who gives no sign of the hurt. In one sense winning is a Pyrrhic victory. To win is to repress. It is also knowing what hurts, and how good timing puts the other lover off guard. In *The Lover* the variations on game-playing have a logic of association. The first lover to vary the game, to carry it into a new dimension and to sustain its conceit, is the winner.

There is also in this sophisticated game-playing a sense of cruelty and desperation. Once the transfer has been made from spouse to lover, the lack of an enshrined relationship means the 'lover' has not one persona, not one identity but several, identities which can be invented, if need be, to infinity. Richard and Sarah find themselves caught in a Faustian trap by their own powers of invention. The temptation of re-inventing themselves as lovers knows no limit. The entry of Richard as Max can be seen as a play-within-a-play, theatrically staged through the atavistic ritual of the drum. But 'Max' is a fragmented invention, a lover who becomes a potential rapist who then saves the besieged wife, as a passing park-keeper with whom Sarah falls instantly in love. In this comedy of enforced errors each lover in turn rejects the other by changing their persona. The cumulative effect of such rejection is to stir the lovers to transgressing desire which is consummated behind the overhanging velvet cloth of the living-room table. But the games which provoke take their toll. When desire explodes it is no longer clear who is making love. The 'lovers' dissolve in the instant of consummation.

The price of marital containment through limitless fantasy is high. Always it is the other self-as-lover through which talk about the spouse is channelled. Pinter here plays ironically on the marital construction of reality. Marriage is often strengthened by the intimate criticism of excluded others, but adultery can turn the weapon of marriage back on itself. If Sarah confides in her lover, then Richard has the right to confide in his mistress. In their fantasy world, hostility is mediated through the other self, painful for them but amusing for us:[4]

SARAH: You talk about me with her?
RICHARD: Occasionally. It amuses her.

SARAH: Amuses her?

RICHARD (*choosing a book*): Mmnn.

SARAH: How . . . do you talk about me?

RICHARD: Delicately. We discuss you as we would play an antique music box. We play it for our titillation, whenever desired.

Pause.

SARAH: I can't pretend the picture gives me great pleasure.

RICHARD: It wasn't intended to. The pleasure is mine.

The couple erect their fantasies of transgression out of a sense of middle-class confidence, feeling they have the space and power to pursue trite games of ecstasy without cost to themselves. To authorise such games is no doubt a gamble. But it is also a manifestation of self-confidence, a belief in their powers of cultural control. They inaugurate an elaborate game of make-believe which mimics the intrigues of actual adultery, but then they gradually lose control. The game they have authorised ends up controlling them. It has in effect, no limit. The 'lover' unlike the spouse has any number of personas. The verbal attack by the aggrieved lover on the absent spouse cannot be contained within acceptable limits, as it will always turn back into the attack of the aggrieved spouse on the unacceptable lover. 'How's your whore?' Sarah asks Richard as he 'returns' from the City, forgetting for a moment as we do that she is describing herself. The game itself becomes elusive and reflexive at the same time. When Sarah tells Max there are other lovers, he cannot know whether they are other personas or other persons, other extensions of himself or other men whose actuality would betray the *raison d'être* of the game. Both know when the game begins, but neither can know when it ends.

   In the end the spouses are prisoners of their own fantasy, unable to distinguish the fantastic from the real. *The Lover* follows the drama of Genet in its dissolution of the boundaries of self and stress on the ecstasy of otherness, but remains closer to *The Maids* than it does to *The Balcony*. It has the tight naturalistic focus on the impersonating couple. Its poetics of space border on claustrophobia. Even the games of seduction which end under the table mimic entrapment. Even the denunciation of game-playing can only be resolved by starting another game:[5]

SARAH: . . .What are you doing, playing a game?

MAX: A game? I don't play games.
SARAH: Don't you? Oh, you do. You do. Usually I like them.
MAX: I've played my last game.
SARAH: Why?
  Slight pause
MAX: The children.

The 'children' are the next game, the biggest cliché, as Pinter realises, in clichéd tug-of-war love triangles. They may or may not exist, but whichever they are they are still invented at a crucial point in the couple's ludic play, improvised into existence by one lover to catch out the other in a charade where invention and injury become inseparable.

The Lover and *The Collection* pave the way for Pinter's greatest dramatic achievement, *The Homecoming*, where he finds a perfect unity of play, sexuality and exclusion. The tragic and comic derive here from the same source, the limits of the will, the delusions of freedom which end in constraint. The disrecognitions which permeate his work are at their sharpest. Pinter, like Shepard, uses the family, the blood-related familiar, as the source of the unfamil-iar. Disrecognition is part of that contempt proverbially bred by familiarity. But only because it is, at the same time, its opposite. It is the refusal to recognise, a perversity which is a source of pain for those who refuse recognition as well as those who are refused it. It is the perverse antibody which rejects Forster's blithely unreal 'only connect'. Disrecognition is part of a vicious circle of injury and anguish which ostensibly denies both. Injury is its cause and anguish its consequence. But the injury and the anguish are largely hidden. For this reason the audience experiences it as comedy. It provokes short spurts of laughter cut dead by an ever tightening dialogue, by Pinter's ability to twist the knife in even deeper. It is the laughter of unease, not of relaxation.

Pinter shares here a concern with family with other Jewish playwrights – Odets, Miller, Wesker. But his techniques of shock differ considerably. In *A View from the Bridge* Eddie Carbone's double kiss is a key dramatic moment. He embraces his step-daughter and then her immigrant boyfriend almost in the same action, involuntarily linking incest and homosexuality in a way which reflects upon his painful ambivalence. Carbone's language is full of rationalisations embedded in the concerns of motive, guilt and moral conscience. In Pinter's characters, on the other hand, the rationalisations of speech are separated out from their moral and psychic sources. Dramatic revelation is not psychic revelation. It is often the opposite. Its revelation is what cannot be fully known. To match this there is an important difference in theme – the absence of the mother. Matriarchal absence, indeed the absence of any female presence, has a strange and eerie quality. The role Ruth will offer to take on at the end of the play echoes the Freudian 'uncanny'. It is an unnerving and outrageous offer which nonetheless strikes a familiar chord, that of filling in the vacuum in the household created by female absence, by the death of Jessie. But it is an offer which subverts all conventional notions of the domestic woman. To that extent, the 'homecoming' is the return of the repressed. Uncannily unrecognised, it dawns amid uneasy laughter with a sense of tragic horror.

The homecoming as return to origin has another overlapping dimension. It is a return to class origins. The play contains a sharp dissection of class power but does not clearly fit into any single class milieu. It is poised uneasily on the edge of the working-class metropolis, divided between the academic couple with children who have moved up and out, and the male kin who have stayed behind. It walks the wire, taut and poised, a supreme balancing act. The family is not exactly proletarian, more *lumpenbourgeois*. Max is a butcher, Sam a chauffeur, Joey a boxer and Lenny a pimp. They exist on the margins of the underworld, seedy entrepreneurs of the city with the inventiveness of the freelance criminal. What unites Teddy with them is family but, it seems, little else. Teddy has risen without trace, a successful professor with wife and kids on an American campus where none would detect his origins. When he goes 'home', his success is disrecognised by his own family, as is Ruth his wife.

At the start Pinter inverts the usual entrances and introductions. He shows us the male family before he shows us their unexpected guests. It is a household where familiarity has bred contempt, where there is little reverence for the dead wife-mother, where homosexual innuendo is the order of the day. Max calls Lenny and later Sam 'a bitch', while Lenny mocks his father's declining powers. Sam's chauffeuring of an American to Heathrow is treated as a pick-up, while Joey, demanding supper, is told to 'go and find a mother'.[6] The womanless household is tetchy, demoralised and potentially vicious. Neither hosts nor guests find what they expect. When the 'guests' meet the 'hosts' the encounter is unorthodox to say the least. When the couple arrive late, Teddy goes to bed without waking his hosts while Ruth, unnervingly, goes out alone for a breath of night air. Teddy disturbs Lenny but tells him nothing of Ruth. When Ruth returns she meets Lenny alone before Teddy has met the rest of the family. The filter of formal introductions is lost. She is 'there' in the house, unprotected.

Lenny's casual greeting is fake recognition of an unknown woman. It changes into fake disrecognition when Ruth tells him she is Teddy's wife. Her person, her figure, her body is 'recognised' before her status is known but her status goes unrecognised once it is revealed. She is thus Teddy's 'woman' and by contemptuous inference, just about anybody's woman, which is why, out of the blue, amidst all his verbiage about Venice, Lenny asks to hold her hand. Pinter plays on the courtesy of first meetings which politely allow name and status to have a spatial reserve that should not be infringed. The social convention of first meeting is clear. Relationships which may deteriorate in the course of time start off from the premiss of dignity and mutual recognition. Here there is neither. But if Lenny can play games of reversal so can Ruth. The tension in the dialogue which follows is as electrifying as anything Pinter has ever written.

Before we look at this more closely we have to see why Pinter is so effective here. If he is reversing social conventions, he is also reversing dramatic ones. By tradition, stage melodramas often 'introduce' us to innocent characters who turn out to be villains. Thrillers make us at home with those who are murderers. At its best in, say, O'Neill, modernist melodrama presents us with the 'front' which has to be exposed, the revelation of moral blemish which is at first concealed. In Pinter it is the other way around. Lenny, and then Max first thing next morning, both make clear they think Ruth is up for grabs, that she is anybody's, a 'smelly scrubber', a 'stinking pox-ridden slut'. Later they come to 'accept' her as Teddy's wife. The insults are calculated and vicious, the response cool and poised. Ruth refuses to rise to the bait. She treats them as if they had never been uttered. Her silence shows a forbidding unconcern. The way is clear for the abuse to be forgotten.

In the encounter with Lenny, she shows she can beat them at their own game. The story Lenny tells, like Hamm's story of the Christmas child in *Endgame*, may well present a 'version' of the listener as its central figure. The 'pox-ridden' woman Lenny claims has propositioned him could well be a fantasy version of the promiscuous middle-class woman he sees in Ruth. His sadistic treatment of her in the anecdote, where he casually beats her up in the tunnel by the docks, is told in a cheerfully callous manner. It is clearly meant to intimidate, to cause fear in the listener. But Ruth not only holds her ground. She adds an unexpected coda to the brutal fantasy. She makes herself an active predatory version of the woman Lenny has dared to insult her with, turning menace back on its perpetrator. Lenny is caught off guard. Her first response to the story, in which Lenny claims the woman is diseased, is to casually enquire how he knows. Later, in the glass of water incident, where Lenny tries to force her to return the glass, she turns the tables more decisively:[6]

LENNY: . . . Just give me the glass.
RUTH: No.
   Pause.
LENNY: I'll take it, then.
RUTH: If you take the glass . . . I'll take you.
   Pause.
LENNY: How about me taking the glass without you taking me?
RUTH: Why don't I just take you?

The challenge only works in context, timed perfectly to counter what has gone before. The neat timing is Pinter's but also Ruth's. It is a feature of Ruth's game-playing. It is also a feature of Pinter's flair for exact tension. Lenny has tried to land all his best shots in his two long anecdotes about assaulting the two women. When he tries to follow this up by taking back Ruth's glass, the dramatic effect is one of overbalancing and leaving himself exposed. It is as if the great effort he expends must have some pay-off. But Ruth refuses to flinch and catches him precisely in his moment of weakness. She has played the game, *his* game, better, because she has counter-attacked with greater economy. The riposte is a metaphorical knee in the groin. It stops Lenny dead in his tracks. It shows us how language can be used to counter the violent threat, something which Pinter himself had learnt as a young Jew confronted in the East End of London after the war by Mosley's fascists. Thus Pinterian language 'contains' violence in a double sense. It contains the threat of violence on the part of the aggressor. But it also absorbs the threat of violence through the counter-attack of the defendant who refuses to be a victim, whose language must contain a plausible counter-threat.

In the play family intimacy is the constant subject of casual derision. Lenny casually asks his father to describe the night of his own conception, to flesh out his image of his parents' fertile copulation. Max recalls being bathed and 'dandled' by his father and later recalls doing the same in turn to his own sons. There are casual undertones of sexual abuse. Max chides Sam about seducing 'lady customers' on the back seat of his boss's car, but in Sam's denial, the subtext is not the rejection of the act but of the gender. Later Max suggests just as casually that Sam would bend down for 'half a dollar' on Blackfriars Bridge. The homoerotic overtones in the household of men without women are brutal and always pejorative. Banter consists of a deliberate wounding of sexuality, of constant slurs on sexual prowess which offset sexual boasting. At the same time as he insults all his family, including his dead wife Jessie, Max waxes sentimental over love and marriage, telling Ruth he has begged his sons each to marry 'a nice feminine girl with proper credentials.'[7]

The sentiments of love and loyalty, marriage and kinship are always echoed at an inappropriate moment. They are undermined by the dramatic turn of events, but equally by the dramatic turn of phrase. At the start of the second act, Max delivers his glowing eulogy to family life, only to end on a note of savage bitterness, 'a crippled family, three bastard sons, a slutbitch of a wife.'[8] He laments his absence at the hasty marriage of Ruth and Teddy the day before their departure for the States, claiming he would have given a white wedding for a 'charming' bride. But Ruth instantly undermines the image of the wonderful bride by claiming she was 'different' when she met Teddy first. After Lenny and Teddy joust over philosophy she echoes the difference in a deft parody of philosophical speech. She refers neither to God nor to the table, those stock-in-trade examples Lenny has been using. Instead she refers to the movement of her leg and the underwear 'which moves with me'. 'Why don't you restrict . . .' she asks them, 'your observations to that?'[9] The taunt is clear. She invites observation to become obsession. She knows they would rather look at the underwear on her moving thigh than talk about philosophy. In order for it to work, however, her challenge has to mimic their speech. She shows she has mastered their discourse and turned it to her advantage.

Later, alone with Lenny, she mentions her life as a 'model for the body', by implication for pornographic photographs. The statement is taut and oblique, a sparse account of the journey to the house and lake at which the pictures were taken. As Teddy comes down with their suitcases for departure, he demands to know what Lenny has been telling Ruth. To the audience, the irony is clear. The husband expects the brother to be making a play for his wife. He does not expect Ruth to be the one who is speaking, who is enticing Lenny with an evasive truth. The spaced disrecognitions which Pinter has orchestrated up to that point are suddenly brought to a climax. Instead of leaving with Teddy, Ruth stays for a 'last dance' with Lenny. As they start to embrace, Joey and Max return in one of Pinter's well-timed entrances. 'She's wide open', Joey exclaims. He takes his turn with Lenny's consent. As she lies beneath him on the sofa, Ruth seems literally to have become family property, just like the sofa itself. She is an object to be shared by all.

Max's speech to Teddy as Ruth lies beneath Joey, a mute object, a still life, is another piece of superb irony. He shows Teddy the courtesy and enthusiasm we equate with homecomings, but only as Teddy is about to leave. He at last compliments Teddy on his wife but only as she is now shared sexual property and will not be going with him. While he refers to Ruth as a woman of quality and feeling, she and Joey roll off the sofa onto the floor. The scene is a tragicomic rendering of scopophilia. The resurgent sexual power of Lenny and Max come from seeing Joey making love to a woman who seems nothing better than a corpse. It is to watch and talk as if nothing were happening. Later, it is to imagine a future for her as if she were nothing more than an object to be disposed of at will. At the same time the thrill involves open friendliness towards Teddy while he secretly and helplessly watches the loss of the woman he loves, to invite him to stay with the family as if it were a cosy and natural thing to do, knowing that staying for him and watching his wife as shared object would be the worst humiliation of all. In the play's most amusing episode, Teddy gains ritual revenge by eating Lenny's cheese roll in exchange for his wife

The cheese roll is little in itself, basic and unappetising. But it becomes a shock commodity. It exchanges for a cherished human body. Teddy's casual insolence in eating something his brother has carefully made to eat himself mimics the family's casual seizure of the woman Teddy has ceremonially taken as his own. The comic imitates the unspoken. For Teddy has moulded Ruth just as Lenny has made his cheese roll and just as Teddy has deliberately eaten the roll so Lenny has 'devoured' his wife. We see here the depth of the suppression of emotion in Pinter's work. Lenny derides his brother as 'a bit inner', knowing that for Teddy openly to plead for her would be a sign of weakness. Because Ruth has made the decision, he cannot take her back without force. But he cannot take her back that way at all since his married life with her has been based on escape from the very culture which condones violent revenge and force. It is not that he is scared to break the rules of the game, but the games he now plays have different rules. To fight physically for Ruth is to play a different kind of game which involves possibly sacrificing the position he has fought for in an academic world. To fight would be to break with his own game and, moreover, probably not win. To plead emotionally or rationally is to belong to a different world. He is in a situation where his powers of philosophy cannot apply. He cannot turn back. Although he has come home, there can be no homecoming.

It is Ruth for whom there is a genuine homecoming, a coming home to family which is not her own, whom she has never seen before in her life. This is something the watching Teddy himself senses. Here Pinter effectively mixes the uncanny with disrecognition. She is doing what he fails to do, and doing it by proxy. Teddy's 'home' is familiar to her as part of the locale in which she grew up. She is attracted back by the challenge of a struggle for sexual power which makes no concessions to respectability. Marriage, campus and family life in America have become sterile, echoed in her description of the country as all rock and sand. The first scene with Teddy slots into place not as the kind of unpleasant encounter she wishes to forget, but the kind of challenge she wishes to re-learn. Pinter, here, offends bourgeois sensibility. Unfortunately for the playwright's detractors he never reduces Ruth to the stereotype of the 'tart' she threatens to become. Her choice is between a life which is comfortable but sterile, and one which is dangerous but challenging, which is more familiar. In the latter the struggle for power is more urgent and more alive.

That struggle already exists in front of us. The men begin to elaborate on the casual offer in which Ruth is to be pimped as a prostitute and turned into a household slave to satisfy sexual and domestic needs. But she drives a hard bargain and preys on their uncertainties. The 'homecoming' will only work on her terms, which her would-be keepers are too weak and uncertain to refuse. Her willing return to the underlife of the city shocks even those who make the offer. The tableau of the last scene with Max collapsed and kneeling before her, Joey's head on her lap, and Lenny at a distance watching suggests her as an authority figure, a matriarchal centre of power. Her role, though, is a travesty of the traditional matriarch. She is erotic, sensual, ruthless, distant and cool. She can 'be' any of the things she wants to be. The role she creates for herself is to enact roles. She may have replaced Jessie, but she has also scrambled the roles of kinship into total confusion. The husband and two brothers all desire her and yet she has outmanoeuvred them all. She is Pinter's one intruder who will come to take over, but only because her intrusion is a 'home-coming'.

Old Times and *No Man's Land* are chamber pieces which retain the complexity of the earlier plays but lack their vitality. *The Homecoming* remains Pinter's most powerful play because it ends on a note of unexpected transformation, neither restoring the status quo nor destroying it in a predictable way. It can be compared, as Orton did, to *Entertaining Mr Sloane* which also ends with outrageous sharing. But English tragicomedy becomes stabilised in the seventies by reference to its bourgeois identity. Middle-class loss is discreet, stifled and comic. It is never total and it is playful in a diminished sense. *The Philanthropist*, *Old Times* and *No Man's Land* are all chamber pieces, modulated renditions of offbeat performance. Nonetheless there are important elements of shock in them which suggest a new kind of attack on middle-class convention. The sexual politics of Pinter's work is never didactic, but it still shatters all complacencies. He broadens the bisexual themes of the earlier work by using memory, and the invention of memories, as a power-resource, a weapon in the struggle for possession.

Old Times shows us a sparer style than the work of the previous decade. The exchanges of dialogue are spare and tense. The longer speeches of Deeley and Anna are memory-speeches, studied recollections which may or may not be true. Each speech contests the memory of the other. The past becomes the key to the present just as memory, and the inventions of memory, become the key to sexual possession. Deeley's desire to protect his wife is flawed by his anxiety that Anna has been his wife's lover. Moreover, she has the more impressive power of recall. His powers of invention never match hers. The more he tries to turn the tables by inventing a past in which Anna has already met and wanted him, the more he is drawn towards defeat. Memory is a contest, a static game for possession in which territory occupies time rather than space. Anna, who appears at first as a joint hallucination of the couple, soon becomes as real as either of them. Yet because there is no certainty about the past, because neither Anna or Deeley can reclaim it triumphantly at the expense of the other, it is a game neither can win. Pinter's achievement is not merely to undermine male heterosexual confidence with the revelation of the affair, but to undermine all confidence in sexuality and any kind of truth about the past.

In *No Man's Land* the contest over the past is also a contest over women, but no women appear in the play. In the homosexual ambience of Hirst's Hampstead home, they are its crucial absence. The shock effect is the contrast between the two, but also the link. Spooner, the outsider, and Hirst, the owner, joust for sexual reputation among men by their memory-accounts of women, whom they both desire and fear. Pinter links the theme of outsider/insider with its intimations of physical violence so marked in *The Caretaker* to the ludic memory-contest of *Old Times*. But the second act seems curiously static as if the protagonists are duellists standing their ground and refusing to budge. There is a loss of dramatic movement and happening in both these plays for which the repertoires of memory, however amusing, however chilling, do not fully compensate. One feels too there is a cushioning effect in these two plays, as if survival was not a matter of desperation, as if the insult to sexuality, though powerful, would never destroy any of the offended characters. Certainly pain and suffering are still there, especially at the end of *Old Times*. But its turbulence has lessened, so that Pinter's ability to explore the extreme ranges of tragicomedy suffers as a result. There are no real outsiders. Everyone, even the seedy Spencer, seems included, and Pinter's dramatic tension occasionally loses its edge or ends up as self-parody.

In the cinema, Pinter's collaboration with Losey shows a similar predicament. The class antagonisms of *The Servant* are much stronger than those of *Accident*. While both are major British films of the sixties the former is the greater achievement. In *The Servant* the linking of class and sexual power is illuminated by a probing sinuous camera which devours the studio space between its characters and moves amongst them with a lyrical and tactile agility. Sexual sharing is ominous and unforbidding as the strategy of a servant couple determined to dominate its masters. In *Accident*, on the other hand, the glacial dissection of bourgeois mores is curiously static, a series of ingenious set-piece confrontations. Pinter's ludic ingenuity is as strong as ever in the tennis match, the aristocratic version of the Eton wall game and the college cricket match, but the sexual intrigue and power-struggles are too formulaic. There is too little at stake, and too little to be lost.

The same is true of Christopher Hampton's bourgeois comedies. The loss is contained, the ambivalence of liberal conscience always to the fore. After the initial suicide of Philip's student in *The Philanthropist* there is always a safety net which protects, which allows life to continue. The tone is acerbic, the irony beautifully restrained. But the matter of life and death is always elsewhere. Hence the greater dramatic power which Hampton manages to generate in *Savages* where the question of fate is played on a broader, more epic canvas, where the fate of West, Carlos and the Indians are of global importance. The loss of shock in Pinter resolves itself in two different ways. In *Betrayal*, he creates a memory-play where the constant shifting backwards of the action in time gives his work a dynamism it had begun to lose with *Landscape* and *Silence*. At the same time this Proustian device allows his characters to assume greater and more conventional definition. Disrecognition is played out, exhausted, discarded perhaps because in *Old Times* it had come dangerously close to self-parody. Instead there is a clear knowledge, of betrayal and its many species, to be had. It is a knowledge as elusive, as multifaceted as anything Pinter had previously written. But the constant movement backwards in time ending with the start of the affair is a quest for discovery, like Proust's of the source of suffering.

The Proust screenplay he had written for Losey in the middle of the seventies contains a sense of memory far more extensive than in his previous work. He used Proust to put back into dramatic memory what Beckett, utterly transforming Proust, had taken out. If memory is deceptive, it still retains what counts. The scenes in *Betrayal* are the same. They are the key moments in the chequered history of a triangular affair which cuts both ways. But Pinter, like Proust, realises that there is no omniscient vantage-point to memory. Any instant can be an instant for reflection on the past only to become part of the past itself with the passage of time. The

Proust screenplay shows both the power and limit of Pinter's vision. After the treatment of Marcel's childhood and Swann's passion, Pinter focuses almost symmetrically on interlocking networks of desire and betrayal, all of them bisexual. His Marcel is the point from which betrayal and desire emanate outwards in opposite directions, male and female, and then joined to form concentric circles around him through a symmetrical formation of same-sex and other-sex liaisons. Morel 'belongs' to the Baron de Charlus but also to Lea, Andrée and their lesbian friends. Albertine betrays Marcel with Andrée but also flirts outrageously with St Loup who has married Marcel's first love, Gilberte.

In Proust the Narrator attempts to exorcise the wounds of betrayal by fusing Reason and Emotion in memory. But in the screenplay, without the reflexive voice, there is no vantage-point from which Marcel can escape the vortex of betrayal. Marcel becomes a figure without knowledge, blind and confused, baffled and beaten. Time is never regained, and instead of Proust's eloquent rationalisation of his Narrator's suffering, we have in Marcel's total failure the evocation of a zero with its own strange and uncanny perfection. In *Betrayal*, Pinter pursues something of the same strategy and makes it work cleaner with only one triangle, in which the cuckolded husband secretly loves his wife's lover more than he does her. The 'betrayal' is not so much the betrayal of lovers for their respective spouses, not Emma's betrayal of Robert, so much as Jerry's betrayal of Robert. Since both men commit adultery, there is no one injured party. The betrayal is also betrayal of the love which dare not speak its name. The play unpeels the developing knowledge of the betrayal, showing, as only Pinter can do, how knowledge develops before it is confirmed by others.

The emphasis on betrayal is on cultural control, the mastery of situations, the discreet power of duplicity. Although, naturally, there are victims and victimisers, Pinter moves into the realms of a serious drama where the world has a greater firmness, a greater surety. The shock impact of play is contained. The tragic effects of disrecognising are gone. Erotic intrigue is still an elaborate game but it depends on knowing the score. It is a deadpan display of virtuosity, of corrupt wisdom. This is equally true of other transformations of the tragicomic in recent English drama. Hampton's brilliant adaptation of Laclos's *Les Liaisons Dangereuses* re-envisages the aristocratic life of the *ancien régime* in terms of amusing subterfuges which produce tragic effects. Despite the fleeting silhouette of the guillotine which appears at the end after the Marquise de Merteuil had declared the need to continue with the game, the play emphasises her calming effect and the triumph of the amoral game. David Hare's recent play *The Secret Rapture* does much the same for contemporary Britain, contrasting the cynical audacity of Realpolitik in Thatcher's Toryism with the tragic failures of liberal conscience and misunderstanding. Isobel, the ambivalent sister of Marion, the ambitious cabinet minister, is a tragic version of Philip, the 'philanthropist' of Hampton's earlier 1970 play. Yet her tragic fate arises in farcical circumstances. In both cases conscience is counter-productive because it is never convincing in a world where little conscience exists. Yet by invoking conscience in the didactic way that Hare does, he creates problems for the form. Unlike Hampton he separates his conscientious characters from his farcical ones, and the play is an uneasy mix of conscientiousness and caricature. The tragicomic slips away from him.

The global dimension of terror which is in Beckett and Genet, Soyinka and Fugard, in Hampton's *Savages*, is absent from the new diluted constellation of English tragicomedy. In the latter, cynicism and self-advantage have no need of terror in order to thrive. But that is the world of a privileged class in a stable and privileged order. Pinter's political attempts to engage terror in *One for the Road* and *Mountain Language* entail an abdication of the comic effects of *The Dumb Waiter*. But they shift uneasily between reality and fable. Pinter sets his fables of terror in unnamed countries in the present as John Whiting did in *The Marching Song*. The deliberate vagueness suffers by comparison with *Savages*, *The Island* or *A Play of Giants*, all of which name their countries and reveal circumstance with political candour. Pinter's brevity in these two pieces also reveals a kind of vitiation. If background is bleached out, then dramatic development is truncated. What Pinter lacks is a prehistory for his characters. Of course, this is precisely what tragicomedy breaks down. But the loss of knowledge is necessarily comic. Without comic devices, it appears strangely fortuitous, an evasion on the part of the dramatist. Indeed Pinter's transition to serious 'political' drama shows just how much the loss of history, the failure to name time and place, depends on the comic suspension of disbelief. In his abandonment of tragicomedy this is something which Pinter clearly failed to resolve. In the American tragicomedy of Sam Shepard the dilemma has been resolved, however, by a different kind of development. History is still a disappearing black hole but the characters who have lost it cling on tenaciously to a myth of their origin. The timeless, invented history that is myth is thus vital to history itself.

7
Shepard I: The Rise of Myth/The Fall of Community

Of all the American dramatists who emerged in the modernist renaissance of the sixties, Shepard is the one who has clearly lasted and gone from strength to strength. The power of his text, the sheer linguistic impact of the spoken word makes his plays enduring even on those occasions when the dramatic action is erratic or has no outcome. He is a child of modernist revolt in an age of mass culture, but also a captive to American myth which has given him a strange freedom. While never fully breaking with naturalist convention, Shepard can project the dramatic illusion of vastness, a poetics of space that has no limit, dream-visions which cannot be explained away. The frontiers of territory become the frontiers of mind. Shepard is not a playwright of the city but of the country which lurks on the edges of wilderness or the fringes of the desert. There is in his ludic urging a nostalgia for the play of childhood, but that nostalgia is not pastoral. It is a mythic search for an elusive space quested by those who seek release from the traps of a civilisation choking on its monstrous technologies. Shepard thus strikes a common chord, the desired regress to a lost world of innocence echoed in the fully modern cadences of an overpowering myth. His tragicomedy simultaneously admits the contrary notions of such an impulse, its comic folly and its tragic consequences.

He is part of what John Lahr has called the search for a new mythology in the American theatre of the sixties,[1] and which found its most potent theatrical charge in the Living Theatre's four-hour spectacle of the Edenic quest, *Paradise Now*. The Living Theatre project a utopian attempt to eliminate history and replace it with a myth of regeneration, linking the deep yearning of pastoral ideal where technology has vanished with the shallow ideal of a limitless sexuality where the self is dissolved in euphoric ecstasy and the audience participates in the general pandemonium. Shepard did not make this mistake. His is the cool fractured theatre of distancing where identification with a mood or an emotion is separated from identification with a character or a community of actors. His plays give us characters who perform action and emotion, not actors who are asked to perform character. His anti-heroes act out obsession in controlled flurries of self-dramatising. Theirs is a virtuoso street-wise solipsism, the product of a saturated drugs culture where heady impulse is ground down by fate, the elongated trip-wire pulled by circumstance. It is also a paranoid world where the self fears the other, the inner soul fears the outer persona, and where, amidst total chaos, the 'unseen hand' is at the back of everything.

Shepard's early work shares with his contemporaries of fiction a concern with the primal horror of contemporary America. In his work and in the best American fiction of the period we find an inversion of that bland invocation of 'the good society' by Lyndon Johnson so quickly drowned in racial insurrection, counter-culture revolt, and the trauma of Vietnam, and soon to be followed by Watergate. *Icarus's Mother, La Turista, Action* and *Operation Sidewinder* parallel *The Crying of Lot 49, Dog Soldiers, Slaughterhouse-5* and *Apocalypse Now* in their grim parodic mocking of a world of fear and greed, in their paranoid evocation of war and surveillance technologies out of control. The common vision of apocalypse here in Shepard, Pynchon, Stone, Vonnegut, Coppola and others is one which matches innocence against corruption, chaos against conspiracy, technology against the makeshift paradise of the tripping and the stoned. Yet these opposites are never truly opposites, never real alternatives, no longer the solid pillars of good melodrama. They are all inextricable, intertwined and finally inseparable. The fate of fusion awaits the unsuspecting play of opposites. Chaos mingles with conspiracy, innocence merges with corruption. Technology invades the illusion of paradise.

Shepard's technique is to shock, to stun, to overturn convention. His characters are voices whose language is poetic but estranging. Yet he also works within the fabric of myths which are substituted for American history. Like Kopit's *Indians*, his work shows the two to be inseparable. As soon as the present becomes the past it runs the danger of being mythologised to provide instant nostalgia and instant heroes. Shepard himself is not averse to myth, and is in no sense a demythologiser. In *The Unseen Hand* he comically juxtaposes the myth of the West against the myth of outer space amidst the junk car culture of an 'accidental town' in Southern California.[2] What we have instead of reverence, however, is a 'making strange' of myth, a series of alienation-effects which wrench it out of its nostalgic niche in the collective consciousness. Nowhere is this clearer than in *Operation Sidewinder* where Shepard repudiates the arcadian separation of technology and nature and forges new myths out of their hybrids. The main hybrid in this case is an Air Force computer built as a rattlesnake which has been programed to track UFO's, and has now escaped into the desert. Micky Free, the Indian, is a human hybrid, the betrayer of his people whose lands he has sold to the Air Force but who is now engaged in rebellion against those with whom he has collaborated. Black and white militants aim to lace the local reservoir with dope and entice stoned fighter pilots to desert with their planes to an obscure Caribbean island. The element of self-parody is deliberate as Shepard indulges in cartoon apocalypse.

At the end the element of melodrama is even stronger than parody. As the Indians reclaim the sidewinder for their snakedance, changing it from a symbol of destruction into a symbol of rebirth, they are invaded by the military hoping to recapture their escaped icon. The confrontation is one of good against evil with Micky, Honey and the Young Man now ranging themselves on the side of mystic purity against military evil. It is a sign of Shepard's imagination and of its limits. Many of his good plays, *Geography of a Horse Dreamer*, *Seduc'd*, *Angel City* and here *Operation Sidewinder*, end in climactic excess as alienation-effects give way to dramatic overkill. It is part of Shepard's dramatic heritage, here honed down to the savage shoot-out which is all performance, in which we cannot tell if anyone actually dies. The machine-gun bullets of the Desert Tactical Troops fail to stop the Indians. The Troops appear to have poisoned themselves by seizing the snake's head while the Indians continue to chant in ecstasy. The sky goes blinding white and then black, an Apocalypse with No Name.

With his send-ups of Neanderthal militaries like Captain Bovine and of the CIA Shepard is indulging in obvious and at times facile parody. With the conversion of the rebels to the mystic purity of the Indians, he gives us a version of easy utopia he elsewhere mocks, and which certainly lacks the resonance of Kopit's historical drama. In a sense the play is too political, too close to the contemporary stereotypes of Chicago in 1968, fleshing out cartoon sketches of radicals and reactionaries in ways that are too obvious. It undercuts its dystopian horror of war technology out of control with the counter-culture's wish-dream of mystic ecstasy. It is an acerbic coda to the writings of Marcuse, Laing, Roszak and Norman O. Brown, but it is also prey, like *Apocalypse Now*, to the attraction of special effects which the most sophisticated forms of death technology can bring to screen and stage. It is perhaps no coincidence that unlike most of Shepard's work which has circulated from off-Broadway to off-off-Broadway, this was premiered at the Lincoln Centre in 1970, an acceptable though never successful version of counter-culture spectacle. But as a playwright Shepard is infinitely better when he opts for an economy of scale.

Shepard's work from 1965 to 1975 also concentrates on the pain of displacement, forcing it out dramatically through short, sharp shock. In plays like *La Turista* and *Geography of a Horse Dreamer* the shock of displacement shades over into disrecognition. Cody in the latter play, Kent and Salem in the former, are all disoriented, losing all sense of where they are, captives in foreign countries who have lost their sense of place and their sense of being. The diarrhoea that is the tourist disease of *La Turista* is echoed in the crabs infection of *Red Cross*. Disease is an affliction which strikes not only at the body but also at the soul, increasing the sense of powerlessness experienced by the frail and brittle self, increasing the power of the 'unseen hand' that is central to Shepard's vision. Bodily illness becomes a catalyst to psychic vulnerability. It deteriorates finally into paranoia, the watchful, frenzied mistrust of an alien world. The dream and drug visions of Shepard's characters take illness into fantasy dimensions. But as the inner world of the imagination expands, the outer world of illness and threat goes out of control.

In *La Turista*, Kent's amoebic dysentery is offset by extreme sunburn, pincer movements of tourist affliction from those moving from north to south. The constant trips to the toilet, the graphic description of the effect of burning on the skin are shock effects which match the patronising attitude towards the locals – and towards all those with darker skin. Kent and Salem in effect suffer for their racial arrogance, but for Shepard the relationship of Mexico and the United States, tourists and locals, is symbiotic. The local boy enlisted to get them medical attention is contemptuous of them as Americans but fascinated by Americana which he assumes to be superior to his own culture. He talks to them in his own version of American slang, obviously copied, a crude imprint of the cultural imperialism they represent but now turned back upon themselves. The scene where Kent is treated by a witchdoctor with the blood of beheaded chickens while Salem develops his symptoms is acted out like a tourist nightmare, a horror vision of being helpless before native superstition. The second act complements the irony, though not with the same success, by projecting Kent back into his native country during the period of the Civil War. The witchdoctor, played by the same actor, has become a quack doctor of his own culture. Shepard plays on the ideology of primitivism and the paranoia of modernity, on the fear of being displaced in space and time and of dying in a foreign land.

Most of his early plays are fantasy melodramas launched from a platform of sharply realist convention and naturalistic manner. The idiom of language, the obsessions of his characters, are poetic adumbrations of Shepard's own culture. Shepard is, like Pinter, a sharp and studied observer of his social world. With equal daring, he lays bare all its conventions. Yet unlike Pinter, he is prone to celebrate excess. Shock effects force action to, at best, transcend its natural plane, at worst betray it. The United States for Shepard is a self-dramatising and melodramatising culture. His characters perform to the hilt and damn the consequences. And yet amidst the humour of their deranged vision and impossible dreaming is the tragic effect of a displacement which destroys. Here Shepard maintains his links with Beckett and the European tragicomic tradition, not on an intellectual plane but a dramatic one. Tragicomedy in the early work is at its strongest where the sense of loss outweighs the excess of fantasy, where the loss is markedly social in its widest sense, the loss of a potential world. One can make a division here between the communal tragicomedies of the early period and the family tragicomedies of the later period. *Icarus's Mother*, *The Tooth of Crime* and *Action* all give us the displaced community of peers. *Curse of the Starving Class*, *Buried Child*, *True West* and *Fool for Love* give us the displaced family from the South West or the mid-West. All are, in some way, excluded or displaced, bemused and bewildered, desperate and paranoid. In his early work Shepard challenges the complacencies of the adult peer-group. In his later work he deconstructs the nuclear family. Both are done with devastating effect.

The early tragicomedies link the shock effects of upended conventions and overturned moralities with the paranoid fear of a world perceived to be hostile and threatening. Shepard is at his best when accurate at targeting convention and controlled in his intimations of apocalypse. *Icarus's Mother* was his third play, written at the age of twenty-three. Its dialogue does not yet have the high-voltage shock of *La Turista* which came out in 1967. But it remains one of Shepard's most powerful and haunting pieces. It is about the loss of past, the barriers to connection, the perverse power of the imagination to be at its most inventive the furthest away it is from actual knowledge. Shepard's five characters are a cross between the average ebullient Americans of Wilder's *Our Town* and the waiting junkies of Gelber's *The Connection*. The Fourth of July Fireworks they anticipate are a ritual fix. What excites their anticipation is not the meaning of the occasion but their attendant sensations, the sight and sounds of the explosions. Between spectacle and meaning there is no obvious connection. After the heavy eating of their barbecue picnic, the group aim to get high on spectacle. As the play opens they see a jet making trails high in the sky.

Like Godot, the jet pilot in the sky is an absent presence, invisible within his vapour-trailing machine. The group make of him what they want to make of him, but do so out of a mixture of awe and fear. Theirs is a visionary speculation which verges on terror, the terror of what they cannot control. Their wild, excited, contrary attempts to read all the signs of the plane's movements are impromptu means of 'recognising' an object which threatens. By reading its intentions, and the motives of the pilot, they hope to pre-empt and ward off the primal fear of disrecognising. There is no settled distance between themselves and the machine. They must be 'near' in order not to be too far. It is as if for the picnickers all distance is a hallucinatory chasm between their collective self and the world, a drug vision which oscillates between elation and horror. Yet Shepard naturalises this horror. He presents us with the relaxed banter of a group of picnickers celebrating a national festival, yet starting to force the pace with the excitement of the moment. It is as if they want to create a happening to match the occasion, yet feel, finally, that the happening has created itself.

The collective act of imagination is inspired: communication with a pilot thousands of feet up in the sky. The motive is dark and shadowed, the fear that failure to do so bespeaks an ominous fate. The lightness of the banter fantastic offsets the darker brooding fear. Pat and Jill present themselves as the pilot's 'two wives', Frank, Howard and Bill as their earthly captors punishing him for his neglect: he is raucously accused of 'running out on you kids!'[3] They project onto him an instant fantasy, an existential accusation which, however absurd, chillingly brings him to life. The tone is amusing but the desperation is strong. The playful fantasy is real in its consequences. Shepard plays on the word 'trip' for the fate of those who go down to watch the fireworks by themselves. They might 'trip' on the beach and become 'unconscious' for weeks. They all prevent Patsy from going to the beach to see the fireworks in case she 'trips' alone. The firework display, Frank warns her, would not be a shared experience which is clearly 'out there'. It could, by implication, be purely a 'trip' of the imagination with 'the sky all lit up with orange and yellow and purple and gold and silver lights.'[4] Shepard's invention is not, melodramatically, to reduce the real to the fantastic, but to suggest that in a drugs culture there is no clear boundary between the fantastic and the real, no clear definition of either. Each of the picnickers has their vision of what the plane does and what it means grounded in the actuality which each vision surpasses. For each vision is apocalyptic. The end of the plane signifies wholesale destruction.

When Howard challenges the group's paranoid fantasy that the pilot can see and hear them while travelling at such great speed and height, his attempt to look at things from the pilot's point of view spills over into an even greater paranoid fantasy. He takes the role of the pilot in the cockpit and literally becomes him. As he tries to explain to Pat the nature of flying, the more he tries to insert himself into the head of the imaginary pilot. The chronicle becomes more frenzied. As he speaks, he moves up close behind her. His imaginary pilot who is now himself becomes dizzy with vertigo. His closeness to Pat's body suggests a masturbatory fantasy running out of control. His wish to become the other has led to deranged exhaustion. But this is merely a spur to consecutive visions. They make smoke signals to attract the pilot's attention. Pat and Jill wave and blow kisses at the low-flying plane after they go to urinate in the bushes and claim the pilot answers with a series of spins and dives. By way of counter-response they lie on the beach and kick their legs in the air, then run naked into the water. According to Pat, lying on her back and staring at the sky, the plane climbs back up to high altitude and writes on the sky with its vapour trail, 'E equals MC squared'.[5]

But Frank has another vision, which is chillingly connected to their equation even if it contradicts their vision. For him, the plane has already crashed to produce 'a recognised world tragedy of the greatest proportion and exhilaration'.[6] It has outrivalled the firework display and the disaster of the Hindenberg. It is the nuclear fear become real but prompting people to regard it as a spectacle, not to flee but to come from miles around to witness its terrible wonder. As Frank speaks, the fireworks start but his own vision has made him oblivious to them. His vision of a nuclear explosion 'an eruption of smoke and froth and flame blowing itself up over and over again' has taken over the firework display and cast it in its own image. The Fourth of July has become Armageddon. One of the girls returns, reaffirming his claim that the plane has come down with the idle excitement of a tourist on a sightseeing trip. But Howard and Bill are too stunned into silence to listen. Motionless they stand holding hands, facing the audience as Frank staggers off. The contrast between excited curiosity and draining horror, the basic polarity of the play, reaches its climax here in the counterpoising of the two men and the one woman. 'It's fantastic,' Jill claims. 'Get away from the picnic area!' Bill cries. In itself the muddled conflict is darkly amusing. But its effect is tragic. There is no middle way between spectacle and disaster.

Shepard maintains the bafflement and the suspense by never showing us what has happened. The explosion is the elusive off-stage threat which could be either the plane or its nuclear cargo. Yet we do not know that it has a nuclear bomb. There is no separation of the reality and the fear, nor in Shepard's dramatic vision can there be. Hence the cheap melodrama of preventing or failing to prevent the worst is avoided. The worst seems to happen and not happen at the same time. The terror is never specified. Its elusiveness is performed to the point of utter desperation. If this play lacks the physical definition of the other early plays, the physical tasks or the physical pain which make them so clearly action plays, the improvised envisioning of terror by the characters is as strong here as anywhere. The almost hallucinogenic nature of paranoia works because the source of the fear is very real. And the terror lingers.

All of Shepard's early plays presented production difficulties for the alternative theatres out of which they were born. His indifference to character and his stress on role-playing meant that Method acting did not really work. The metonymic structure of his text meant that symbolic elaboration was equally unsuccessful. Many

directors have been candid about the difficulties of directing his
early work, notably Ralph Cook for the Genesis theatre production
of *Chicago*, Michael Smith for his New York production of *Icarus's
Mother* and Richard Schechner for the Theatre Performance
Group's version of *The Tooth of Crime*.[7] To some extent the
improvisational nature of the theatre culture out of which Shepard
emerged in off-off-Broadway worked against the solidity of his
text. For in his work the dynamic chaos of both America and its
counter-culture are transposed into dramatic structure. His distance from character and situation could be cool, if not Brechtian at
times. Audience participation or audience-berating in forms then
fashionable had no place in his work. Neither did empathy. In his
early links to the Open Theatre of Joe Chaikin where he still felt
himself to be marginal, the group focus on Goffman's *Presentation
of Self in Everyday Life* seemed to have had a substantial impact.[8]
Goffman's view of the self as a performing entity which worked
itself out through a succession of instants had its counterpart in the
'transformation' exercises by which actors would change personality from scene to scene in a specific play. Shepard's role-reversals
were later to be swift and spectacular, instances of shock transformation which challenged the whole idea of consistent personality. He quickly became a master at dramatising the transient self in
a transient culture.

Shepard's move from the one-act to the two-act play also shows
a deeper sense of transformative action. In *La Turista* the historical
time-switch of the second act is inventive, but also muddled and
melodramatic, a vitiation of a superb and lacerating first act. Soon,
however, the switch started to work for him, as a marker of the
reversal of fortune and the expanding of dramatic action. In that
respect it is a key feature of *The Tooth of Crime*, *Geography of a Horse
Dreamer*, *Angel City* and *True West*. In all four plays, reversal of
fortune entails a reversal of roles and displays a fertile absorption
of the dramaturgy of *Godot*, one of the few modernist plays to have
an impact on Shepard as a young writer. Whereas Beckett stresses
stasis amidst change, Shepard as a modern American writer
emphasises change amidst stasis. The 'gang' and later the 'family'
are larger units than Beckett's two-handers. The 'gang' is any
community of peers thrown together by circumstance, often
hierarchic but also marked by the egalitarian culture of Shepard's
native land which challenges the hierarchies it creates. Shepard's
communal plays are made up of a 'gang' of disparate people

jostling for position and played by a 'gang' of actors existentially as a series of exercises in performance. This double informality springs both from the contemporary culture and the theatre culture which Shepard knew best. The match is impressive, and it does not exclude the dimension of power. In Shepard's plays we find the equal right to challenge and displace the powerful, but that right is also the right of the hustler, the opportunist, the con-artist, the visionary. It is never obvious until it is taken up.

The *Tooth of Crime*, *Angel City* and *True West* are all about hustler-dreamers on the outside moving in and upwards, while those they displace move down and out. Positions of power do not bring in their wake dignity, decorum or refined culture. Wealth in Shepard's anti-heroes brings no pretension to gracious living but is simply a prop for megalomania and decadence. Cultural power creates its own robot-like rules which can only be avoided as Henry Hackamore does, the Howard Hughes clone of *Seduc'd*, by becoming a paranoid recluse in the Central American jungle and dreaming of returning to Las Vegas. Shepard's success-heroes, and there are few of them, are brittle and vulnerable. Austin in *True West*, Wheeler in *Angel City* and Hoss in *The Tooth of Crime* are all there for the taking by those who use their own methods more ruthlessly. Hoss, in particular, is Shepard's most considered travesty of a Renaissance tragic hero. He has the power, the wealth, the glory, the mansion with its own moat which is the rock star's version of the royal palace. His industry acolytes mirror the king's courtiers and advisers. But he has, of course, no pedigree, no lineage, no noble graces. He is the self-made idol who stands or falls by his reputation, the leader of the pack remote from his fans as a king from his poorest subjects. But he cannot rest on his laurels. His reputation cannot stand still. He has to be a mover, to make more gold records, ever-recurrent kills. All he has in common with a king is a throne.

Even in the matter of the throne, Hoss is closer to Hamm than to Hamlet. Instead of an armchair on castors, he occupies 'an evil-looking black chair with silver studs and a very high back, something like an Egyptian Pharaoh's throne...'[9] But like Hamm's armchair, his throne occupies centre stage, the starting point for an elaborate game he is doomed to lose. Hoss and Crow, his upstart contender, have the same initials as Hamm and Clov but are more like Didi and Gogo in their equal contending of the spoken word. They are programmed into their fractured roles, appearing to improvise in a world of chance but bound by a game of fame which has produced them in its own image. If Hamm cannot move unless pushed, Hoss is by contrast one of Shepard's incessant movers. But in the premature twilight of his fame, he needs a fix before each move, a narcotic raising of his act, an artificial spur to performance. He is the system's version of the lone, unique megastar, a frazzled effigy of Nietzsche's *Übermensch*.

In this play, the most overtly musical of Shepard's opus with its demanding rock lyrics and on-stage music, he continues Beckett and Genet's explorations of human tragedy bereft of selfhood. But he invokes mythic dimensions of American culture far removed from European modernism. The archetype for the conflict between Hoss and Crow is the Western shoot-out, in a decade when that exhausted movie genre had started to shed its concerns with courage and honour. Shepard's format is closer to the bleak and nihilistic commerce of death in Peckinpah's *The Wild Bunch* or Eastwood's *High Plains Drifter* than to the early tortured evocations of honour in *Shane* or *High Noon*. First produced in 1972, it is of the same period of doubt and self-loathing in American life. But instead of the brute melodrama of inexhaustible killing, Shepard treads the opposite route. The shoot-out is menacing but comic, deadly but absurd. It is violent action demythologised. Words, not guns or knives, are the deadliest weapons. The play is neither thriller nor parody, though it comes perilously close to both. It is a tragicomedy hewn out of junk-'n'-junkie culture, a rearguard guide to the survival of the fittest in the dog-eat-dog world of rock-'n'-roll where even the fittest fail to survive. The suicide of Hoss is tragic in its own way, a sudden culmination of long disintegration. What is comic is the contrast between the dream of eternal fame which spurs him into battle and the collapse of body and soul which ensures he will not win. No noble mind or worthwhile body is here overthrown and no gold record is worth the human waste.

Shepard's talent lies in being constantly elusive about the nature of the contest between Hoss and Crow. Fatal encounter is as lyrically indefinable here as apocalypse in *Icarus's Mother*. It is a perfect hybrid made up of a Western shoot-out, a street-car race, a gold-record chart-busting war, a gang fight over turf, a rapping contest and a boxing match. It is all of these things and none of them, a mythic and dialogic encounter whose rules are never clear and are there, anyway, to be broken. It is no wonder that Hoss, after a technical knock-out has been awarded against him, shoots the referee. But if the encounter itself is not judged according to any recognisable rules, that is because the game within which Hoss has become a machine-killer itself has no recognisable code. The code is a commitment to honour the rules but the rules are never clear. They may change from moment to moment. The game has to be played, and Hoss has to go on playing it to outrival all rivals, but the deadly rivals are those, like Crow, who do not acknowledge the code. They play the game to bend the rules, and bend the rules to gain victory.

Surrounded by his entourage, Hoss still feels his power ebbing. Becky, his woman, can no longer convince him of his manhood. Galactic Jack the DJ can no longer convince him the charts are in his favour. Doc cannot cure him of his ailments and is merely there to 'shoot him up' while he laments the passing of the code: 'There's no sense of tradition in the game anymore. There's no game ... Can't they see where they're goin'! Without a code it's just crime ... I think the whole system's getting shot to shit. I think the whole code is going down the tubes. These are gonna be the last days of honour.'[10] But Hoss is also trapped inside the game, in the same way that he is trapped inside his mansion. Having worked his way up, there is no way back. He is cushioned, protected, propped up and helpless. Thus Becky's reaction when he threatens to go on the lam is to tell him that he would not recognise the world outside the game, that he would not 'have a snowball's chance in hell of makin' it'. The streets are controlled by 'gangs and Low Riders', who are controlled by 'cross-syndicates' in turn controlled by 'the Keepers'. The paranoia is like a cross-breeding of gang argot and science fiction. Becky tells me the game is everywhere except for a distant island where 'everybody's on downers all day'.[11] There are no boundaries in which the game can be contained, just as there are no rules. It has become a universal poison.

Here Shepard matches the legacy of Beckett to a paranoid feel for the disintegration of the American Dream. The dialogue echoes that of Hamm and Clov where Hamm demands to know what is outside his bunker, but Shepard naturalises the unspeakable, the abandoned outside through Becky's answers which seem as if they speak from experience, but which cannot specify it, cannot pin it down. The conspiracy theory of control 'of the streets' extends across the nation. There is nothing 'outside the game', meaning that the game outside is far more deadly than the game Hoss already knows. There are no residual spaces left. Hoss's contrary wishes, the craving, on the one hand, for peace in some untouched space where there is no game and the desire, and on the other, to roll back his career and hustle as in the days before fame, are both blotted out by Becky's paranoid projecting of a game-playing now more formidable and far-reaching than ever. Play on the inside is dangerous, but on the outside is fatal. There is no refuge from it anywhere.

Yet the play's attraction, its visceral excitement, comes from its superb rendering of undifferentiated play, the central encounter of Hoss and Crow which cannot be effectively nailed, which defers definition. Here it is the regress of play into childhood which lies behind, and also contradicts the nostalgia for honour and the code. Where child's play is an imitation of the real, or of the myth of the real, it is a rehearsal for the real thing it copies but does not yet know. The adult relationships of Shepard's early plays transform rehearsal into performance without altering the nature of play. His characters, at times, are children in adult bodies. Their play is a form of present-ness doubling as nostalgia, an existential regress into impossible utopia. If Lasch's Americans of the 'me-generation' have failed to outgrow their narcissism, then Shepard's characters have failed to outgrow the fixations of play. They want to act as if they were still children, as if there were no difference between girl and woman, boy and man. In a culture of available sex, casual violence and easy drugs, play alone signifies the return of the repressed, or more precisely, the promise of innocence.

The past is both childhood and myth. Hoss is nostalgic for an authentic age, for the Old West, for the Blues, and for teenage memories. Against this Shepard sets the automatic language of Crow, the machine-killer, the Keith Richard look-alike complete with silver swastika. Suspense turns on the sightings of Crow that are reported, the inevitability of his coming, and the scene at the beginning of Act 2 where he is first seen already seated on Hoss's throne. The sustained high pitch of the action, its deliberate excess, make this a supreme example of American melodrama. Yet its form is modernistic. Hoss is in a game which excludes the honour he nostalgically craves. He is an anti-hero, the sated, prematurely clapped-out rock star waiting to be deposed by someone for whom nostalgia means nothing. The verbal duels between champion and contender pit memory and origin against machine success and nothingness. Shepard's dialogue is at its most inventive in the clash of words that is a clash of styles, yet dialogic in its overflow, in the polyphonic flow of one speech into another:[12]

> HOSS: . . . Are we playin' to a packed house like the keepers all say?
> CROW: (*he cackles*): Image shots are blown, man. No fuse to match the hole. Only power forces weigh the points in our match.
> HOSS: You mean we're just ignored? Nobody's payin' attention?
> CROW: We catch debris beams from your set. We scope it to our action then send it back to garbage game . . .

In Freud paranoia stems from the fear of being watched, of being caught in a sexually compromising act. But in Shepard, paranoia is heightened by the fear of *not* being watched. Hoss's feeling of being 'stuck in his image' is one of being petrified into stone. But what is worse is if it is all for nothing, if the millions of eyes and ears which have held him in that posture are no longer there at all. The greatest terror of all is to be commodified into an image no longer on anyone's retina. Indifference is unbearable to the ravaged narcissist who thinks his game is the only one that counts, and finds he has no audience. Hoss is, to use his own word, 'impotent', one of Shepard's disintegrating figures of authority who finds he can authorise nothing. He is in fact a captive to the game, a product of fame who has been turned into a commodity which is no longer unique and can now be replaced. His replacement here, however, the Pretender to his throne, has no conscious sense of being stuck in his image. He *is* his own image and nothing but an image, a talking machine offloading fractured metaphors.

Hoss and Becky have no self to fall back on once fame deserts them. But they have the power to be aware of their shortcoming, of the hiatus between Self and Image. In sharp contrast, Crow's demonic celebration of the Image is the acclamation of a smooth and polished surface without depth, a figure without origin. He concedes no history to the music he plays. It remains disrecognised, just as he is. He is marked as a Gypsy Killer from Vegas. In other words he has come out of nowhere. While Hoss challenges him with the history of jazz and the blues, Crow is contemptuous of his rival's dependency on the past. He himself moves with the present and has no ancestors. Shepard is perhaps prophetic here of the fate of white rock music, passing through that phase which Crow clearly embodies, of ripping off black rhythm and blues for commercial advantage, to that stage he implicitly foreshadows, the production of gold record music by sound machines. There is a tension, though, in Shepard's created figure between demonism and nullity, between the bird of prey which the name suggests and the programmed devaluation of music language, the hustler's street rap become robot talk. It is a fruitful tension, a sign that no evil is absolute. But the apocalyptic strain is there all the same, the fatal transformation, the sense of mythic loss, the sudden approach of the lacerating disenchantment of the world.

Because of its reliance on live music and Shepard's own lyrics, involving simplified rock progressions and the distinct undertow of The Velvet Underground, the play presents performance difficulties. To the author's knowledge, it has only been staged twice, professionally, in the United Kingdom, the first version by Charles Marowitz being one on which Shepard himself collaborated. Richard Schechner has recorded the pitfalls of his own production with the TPG in New York when he rejected the use of amplified music and adopted a 'verbophysical' approach to the text, choices about which Shepard was very wary.[13] The play demands reverence for both the electronic music and the text and a dramatic integration of both. The irony of the modernist predicament here should not be lost. The most powerful modernist play ever to use popular rock music was, for that very reason, largely consigned to limbo. It ends up being wrongly valued not as a performance but as a readable text 'about' performance. Its fate, in fact, summarises the whole relationship of tragicomedy to performative culture.

Shepard's communal tragicomedies show the centrifugal forces which pull apart the informal group, the hyperactive gang with its brittle hierarchies and lack of family attachment. They point up the weakness of comunal ideals in the decade of counter-culture. Apart from *Operation Sidewinder*, Shepard does not deal directly with the counter-cultural commune or revolutionary *groupuscule* of the period. Yet he does pin down the general dilemma of communal living in an individualistic culture, the conflict between ideals of spontaneous group existence and the egocentric obsessions of the individuals who compose such groups. A drugs culture which breaks down inhibition and nourishes amnesia also encourages the phobic obsessions of the self. Shepard's freelance groups all seem to be free-floating, to have their own *raison d'être*, beholden to no one. Yet they are unknowingly trapped by position and circumst-

ance, culture and history, by a freewheeling version of disrecognised fate. They all appear as free spirits but equally as collective
victims. This is the basic contradiction of recent America so crucial
to Shepard's vision of things. They embody it well. With Shepard
at his sharpest, such a grouping becomes a perfect theatrical
microcosm, thrown into performing its disrecognised fate, into – to
paraphrase one of his characters – 'acting itself out'. That is to say,
it is thrown into consuming itself utterly in performance.

Action and *Angel City* continue the theatre of deranged communalism, the latter with the sprawling melodrama demanded by
its Hollywood theme, the former with the tight and coiled economy of situation which connects so well with Beckett and Pinter.
Action is one of Shepard's shortest plays but also one of his most
powerful. All his major themes are concentrated and purified into a
single and sustained piece of drama whose implosive stasis gives
the play's title its obvious irony. Like Beckett, Shepard can make
everything happen when nothing is happening. The play's recurrent motif, the failure of his four players to find the place in the
book they are taking turns at reading, establishes the zero development. The page they can't find, the story they don't tell, is part of
the life which does not advance. The occasion is Christmas, one of
intimate ritual, but there are no blood relations in sight. The two
men, Jeep and Shooter, and the two women, Liza and Lupe, seem
to have no clear relationship to each other. They are an anti-family,
the remnants almost of a forgotten commune holed up in a remote
farmhouse in the middle of nowhere. Theirs is a residual existence.
Shepard combines the sense of their winter isolation, their remote-
ness from anywhere, with their sense of entrapment within the
walls of their shabby dwelling-place, and their separate imprisonment within their own obsessions. They are slowed still further by
a radical entropy. The basic mechanics of daily living seem to have
deserted them. They know not what they do.

The eating of the Christmas turkey is done without any feeling of
communal good. It is cooked too fast, eaten too quickly and
finished before Shooter can have his portion. After Jeep has
smashed two chairs in separate and violent tantrums, Shooter
seeks out an armchair for him which he claims not to want. By the
time Shooter has remembered his mission, found the chair and
heaved it into the room, the meal is over and he has missed out on
the turkey. The ceremony of eating, as one where all are present, is
grotesquely violated. But then all communal ceremony is physical-

ly travestied. The common link, as well as eating, is the vain task of looking for the place in the book to finish the story they all love. Everything else is private obsession. It has to be said that the central focus here is male. Jeep and Shooter are the deranged drug visionaries of the piece. All Liza and Lupe seem to share with them is their absent-mindedness. The women play a considerable but always secondary part. It is a deficiency Shepard does not redeem until he writes the family tragicomedies. But if they do lack the rampant paranoia of their male counterparts they are in no sense domesticating creatures. Shepard plays powerfully on a total lack of any contact between the sexes that is not mechanical. They do not connect. The women do not act, as is often the case in domestic naturalism, as phony arbiters of the male conscience. Their main posture is one of indifference. Along with much else in the play, that indifference works as a shock that is hard to take.

Disrecognitions of common ritual, sitting, cooking, serving, eating, even dialogue in its literal sense, pepper the inert action of the play. The parodic echo of the counter-culture commune is present in the shiftless dialogue which fails to define any sense of community at all. Shooter has just recounted his narcotic phobia of a friend who was killed by his own body. Lupe contests that no such thing could have happened in the old days of mass entertainment or the community in which she was once active:[14]

JEEP: What's a community?
LUPE (*looking up*): A sense of – a sense, um – what's a community, Shooter?
SHOOTER: Oh, uh – you know. You were on the right track.
LUPE: Something uh –
JEEP: I know.
LUPE: Yeah. You know. It doesn't need words. (*She goes back to her book*)

She then tries to explain that it is a form of mutual self-help but Jeep is no longer listening and no longer cares. The term community cannot be defined because there is no community of speakers and no community of listeners.

It is a classic instance of wires crossed, of comic Shepardian confusion. Jeep is still obsessed by Shooter's phobic tale and demands to know if Shooter's friend had suspected his body of treason. As in Beckett the subject of the tale could obliquely be one of the characters in the play, in this case Jeep himself whom Shooter has disrecognised. For Jeep is someone trying metaphorically to escape from his own skin, the inversion of Shooter's 'friend' whose body has escaped from him and then killed him. He vaguely identifies the fate of Shooter's 'friend' as his own. And yet Shooter's friend could also be Shooter himself, that part of him which has already escaped. For his tale echoes the expression of an earlier phobic anxiety, his fear of looking at the skin which covers his body in the bathtub. The episode is at once amusing and unsettling. In a visionary world out of control the disassociation of body and soul has become frighteningly real. Both men feel themselves to be on the outside of their bodies looking in, to have drifted free as if in the re-enactment of some primal horror.

Towards the end the predicament of the two men has become horrifyingly similar. Yet they can hardly be said to share the predicament. They both feel trapped, inert, encased in a claustrophobic world, yet theirs is not felt as a common fate. It is projected in each case as an egocentric vision. 'Action' becomes the disassociation of actions and finally the disassociation of visions. The narcotic subtext of Shepard can easily appear to get lost in the casual freakiness of monologue. But it is indubitably there. The fix is a false utopia which promises unlimited vision and delivers phobia, anxiety, the shrinking of the whole world into a prison-house. Shooter's tussle with the chair suggests something more than the mere wish to root himself to the spot. It is also the metaphoric abdication of a different kind of travelling, of sniffing around and putting his nose into a desirable dust whose drug meaning the language makes fairly explicit:[15]

> SHOOTER: . . I'd give anything just to travel around this space. Just to lick the corners. To get my nose in the dust. To get my body moving.
>
> LUPE (*referring to book*): Was it near the place where the sky rained fire?
>
> SHOOTER: I can picture it. I give into it. I let my body go. It moves out. It sniffs the boards. My head imagines forests! Chain saws! Hammers and nails in my ears! A whole house is being built!
>
> LUPE (*in book*): Keep it to yourself.

Shepard amusingly mixes metaphors of 'sniffing out' and 'snorting up', both forms of discovery of a kind. But Shooter ends up neither with the soothing calm of stasis or the excitement of imaginary adventure. He is, as he puts it, 'nowhere'. His radical resort to staying put in the chair is a form of giving up on adventure, the pain of losing the prospect of vision but also, by implication, the relief of getting off drugs. The rooted chair which is a metaphor of the human predicament in Beckett becomes here a more specific and more drastic remedy. Shooter's decision not to leave his chair is shock melodrama, as is the failure of the others to recognise the decision. As Jeep starts to bone fish at the table, Shooter tips over his armchair and keeps sitting in it. The two women enter and hang out some washing right across the stage. All three activities suggest a cutting off, the women from the men, the men from one another. Shooter then pulls the armchair over himself with his arms sticking out of the sides and walks around like a tortoise. Nobody pays any attention. He becomes a voice, hidden from view. His new imprisonment is mirrored by Jeep's obsessive account of a real prison he has been in. As Shooter lumbers about hidden from view, Jeep recounts prison nightmares – shades of O'Neill – of walls moving in on him. The space on stage becomes the space of the cell he remembers. Grotesque memory is mirrored by grotesque image, the trap of Jeep's past by the trap of Shooter's chair.

Action gives us the best of Shepard's many bleached-out images of the apocalypse, the wasteland that is both real and imaginary, inside and outside all at the same time. It is in many ways his *Endgame* quartet. The residues of a dying culture are washed up and hardened into precious metal. The play presents us in microcosm with the legacy of an age, an age which had tried to rediscover the American Dream with greater intensity than its complacent predecessors and then failed with a pathos which lurches between catastrophe and farce. It is not so much that the American Dream has died. It is more that the attempts to resurrect it has quickened its ruin. Shepard is aware of the urgent attraction of the Dream as well as the dangers of its easy demise. It is his special talent to fuse the two. It is right too to use a single space which is neither that of family or community, of the remnant *groupuscule* which has neither lineage nor solidarity. In this way Shepard naturalises Beckett's bleak and terminal vision into the plight of his own society in the later part of the twentieth century.

Angel City by contrast works at the extreme edges of melodrama.

Its subject, the urgent saving of a Hollywood film which looks like a commercial disaster, is a melodramatic plot about a melodramatic culture. To that extent, it is comically reflexive. The film-makers behave in the play with the self-indulgent excess of characters in a lurid Hollywood thriller. Yet Shepard traps them into the stage. They are not stars of the silver screen but practitioners of fantasy who exist on the wrong side of the cameras and despair even before the cameras have begun to roll. By playing on the idea of a 'disaster' movie which has become a financial disaster, Shepard probes a sudden and transient genre of the seventies. 'Disaster' is the sub-genre within the genre of melodrama. Yet Shepard wishes to make it clear in this that Los Angeles, the 'angel city', is the centre of the disaster, a city which is doomed to destruction. Where *Endgame* had conjured the performance of apocalypse, Shepard's play spells out the commodification of disaster. The imminent fate of the American West is to be turned into a safe and saleable object. In the city under threat, there is always someone wanting to make a movie about a city under threat, and the humans attempting to save a movie about humans under threat, themselves behave as if they are under threat. And of course they are. For in their 'industry' they are only as good – meaning successful – as their next picture. To make this one sell is to survive. To fail to make it sell is to go under.

As Wheeler edges out Lanx and oozes green slime, he employs Rabbit and his Indian medicine bundles to work some shamanistic magic on his derailed megabuck technology. But in his frenzied urge to justify his own grand ambition he is driven to the same urgent rationalisations as a novice scriptwriter trying to defend his untried project. Rabbit, the real novice, takes full advantage and usurps his place, treating him as the novice and taking over as well the facial horror of his green slime. Rabbit, the outsider, displaces Wheeler, the insider, only to become, literally, bundled into the system. For the system devours the Other as well as its own. On the verge of disaster it is omnipotent. Its leaders and minions alike are equally its victims.

Shepard's gang of film-makers, the dreamy secretary, the drummer brought in to find elusive magic rhythms, the deranged competing producers, the shamanistic outsider, never suggest fixed roles with fixed forms of authority. Authority seems invented as it might be by players acting on a stage. Shepard here is both existential and reflexive. The disaster movie is being made up as it goes along, almost existentially improvised like the jazz motifs which Shepard uses recurrently throughout. At times the self-indulgence takes over, and Shepard's Brechtian distance from his melodramatic theme is lost. Given the subject-matter, it is perhaps inevitable. The hypercharged, frantic, insomniac quality of the action suggests a manic culture awash in cocaine. Unlike many talented film directors of modernist melodrama, however, Shepard is never finally seduced by the lure of melodrama. He keeps his distance from the mayhem of the excess he has created. Such mayhem stems, his words imply, from the most fatuous forms of high-speed vanity whose obverse is fear of total ruin.

Yet his characters in *Angel City* remain paper-thin and rootless. If the play is about the disintegration of myth into commodity, it too loses its hold on the past. Shepard's existential movie gang is lateral in conception, not only existing in the present but also in a cult of the eternal present. It springs out of nowhere and has no longevity. It is stretched flatter and flatter until it is on the verge of disintegration. The turn to family meant not the usual crises of naturalistic drama with a naturalistic psychology to match. It meant the search for lineage as a stronger guarantor of myth, even if that lineage was problematic, even if it was deceptive and self-defeating. The chronology of his change, which started in the mid-seventies, mirrors also the failure of counter-culture and its 'alternate' families, its hyperbolic communities. But in his return to a more conventional form of 'family' Shepard shows us that in his world no such thing exists. Or rather, within the wider plane of American history, it no longer exists even if it once did.

8

Shepard II: The Shock of the Normal

Shepard's turn to the family in the late seventies repeats to some extent the earlier pattern of O'Neill, the move out of a wider social microcosm towards more intense bindings of kinship and the agony of genealogy. Equally, however, the movement away from modern tragedy in its Aristotelian form had by now become total. The European distancing of Brecht and disrecognising of Beckett were things which Shepard had begun to absorb into his distinctively American writing. Yet both had comic and satiric potential which he had not yet fully explored. In *Curse of the Starving Class* (1977), *Buried Child* (1978), *True West* (1980) and *Fool for Love* (1983) he was soon to do so. This he did by finding the new focus on the family which had been absent from much of his earlier work, and which involved a return to convention. Here he seemed to accept a more naturalistic frame of meaning, a more restrictive template of dramatic space. In return, however, he affirmed what Pirandello and Beckett had achieved before him, a modernist rapture which made him closer to Kafka than to O'Neill, a sense of how the horrifying and the barbaric can inhere in the ordinary.

The new unity he forged in the ordinary and the terrifying, a unity which relied neither on fantasy nor the supernatural, was casually subversive. For it denies his familiar subject any fixed form. In the age of the American family as a declining institution, the nature of his new subject, *his* families, is that they never establish themselves as tangible entities. Shepard never tells us what a family is and never proceeds as if its nature can be taken for granted. A priori, its status is problematic, its structure frail, its meaning utterly confused. We no longer have crisis dramas based on conscience and its many betrayals. A more common pattern is for comic and unwitting victims to conspire actively in their own damnation. In *Mourning Becomes Electra* O'Neill mistakenly tried to update the classical tragic elements of curse and doom to nineteenth-century America. In *Curse of the Starving Class* Shepard tries to update them to twentieth-century America. But he consciously makes them funny rather than cathartic, and gets away with it. Rather than react with pity to the misfortune of his characters an audience is more likely to puzzle over them. Rather than react with terror it is more likely to offer up a wry smile at their bewildered plight.

The shock Shepard presents us with in his collapsing families is not the shock of the absurd, but the shock of the normal. If the dramatic effect is one of calculated sensation, then the everyday itself becomes sensational in the best sense of the word. Banality is a form of hubris. The family is neither integral or intense, binding or nuclear. There is no nuclear core guaranteed by relationships of blood. All that is guaranteed is proximity. Shepard duly brings his family members together in a single, enclosed space. Minimal encounters are punctuated by minimal communication. The effect is heightened by melodramatic effects which are distinctively American. At times they can work with devastating power. At other times they create excess clutter or excess frenzy. The dramatic pacing of Shepard's work is sometimes flawed in the last act by his tendency to flood the stage with characters and bombard it with quick-fire, self-indulgent happenings. It is always a risk of melodrama. Yet Shepard in his best work transcends that risk with the finality of unexpected gesture, a showing or display of primal horror at the heart of the normal. He consistently avoids the pitfalls of an easy pathology. One cannot write off his displaced persons as freaky or demented without questioning the structures through which they live and by which they are imprisoned. Most of his work displays a vision of exclusion rather than a judgement of failure. We are asked to be perturbed but not to moralise. Judgement of individual characters, perhaps strangely, becomes pointless.

In *Curse of the Starving Class* and *Buried Child* he expanded his dramas to three acts for the first time to focus on the single family. He then reduced his scope again for the more intense sibling and quasi-sibling contests of *True West* and *Fool for Love*. But in *A Lie of the Mind* (1985), his longest and ambitious work to date, he returns to the three-act format in his study of two separate but entangled families. Here, the novelty is the addition of separate scenes within the acts. This is largely in order to move back and forth between the different family locales. In addition he extends the stage spatially, using split-level scenes with upstage platforms, effects more reminiscent of the stage settings of Williams and Miller. To date, this remains an exception. *Curse of the Starving Class* stays with the single set but starts off with its space already violated. Wesley is attempting to fix the kitchen door which his father has broken down in his drunken attempt to enter the house the previous night. Later the absent door is further complicated by the sheep-pen set up in the kitchen for a farm lamb suffering from maggots. On his next attempt to enter the doorless kitchen with its sheep-pen, Weston is unable to distinguish the inside from the outside. Literally and metaphorically, the house is wide open, there for the taking by the crooks and speculators who want to buy up the farm to develop the land. The farming family of an affluent California have none of the sentimental integrity of Steinbeck's Joads, nor their powers of stoic endurance. But that is because the title is ironic. Even though they never use the refrigerator properly, they are not going to starve. The refrigerator is empty because they are inept, not because they are destitute. The fun starts because the audience already knows it.

In breaking new ground with his family tragicomedy, Shepard returns to more conventional plotting. The drunken father is fleeced by a crook who sells him arid desert land, the witless mother hoodwinked and seduced by a conniving lawyer into selling her rights on the land they jointly own. The dramatic tension openly plays off the outcome. Will they or will they not outwit the predators? But Shepard subverts melodramatic cliché through modernist enactment, the comic and bizarre ways in which the drama of defiance, and lack of defiance, is performed. By acting out conventions, Shepard's characters make a mockery of them. Moreover, Shepard's collapsing family provides no anchor for convention at all. Sporadically defying their predators, they are at the same time disintegrating of their own accord. No family unity can be called on in time of strife. There is no standing shoulder to shoulder. There are instead a series of transient and glancing encounters, more accidental, it often seems, than deliberate. No one in this isolated and besieged family seems to know when they might see someone else. And no one seems to care.

As in *Action* Shepard reaffirms the separateness of male and female, and emphasises it in the paired similarity of gender names, Ella and Emma, Weston and Wesley. But there is no solidarity of mother and daughter, father and son to compensate. As Wesley re-enacts his father's drunken tussle with the door in his all too vivid imagination, his unlistening mother is already enacting her maternal advice on menstruating for Emma, who has just started having periods. Here she has started her inane lecture even before Emma enters the room. 'I want you to know all the facts before you go off and pick up a load of lies. Now the first thing that you should never do is go swimming when that happens. It can cause you to bleed to death. The water draws it out of you.'[1] It is a comic alienation-effect to show the lack of contact, the purely ritual and token nature of the admonition which continues once Emma is there arranging her chicken-cooking charts. As the action goes on, pretty soon the family becomes an insane asylum in a heartless world.

The refrigerator is the family's fifth member – at one point Emma speaks to it lovingly at great length. It is the nodal point of connection between the family members which shows up their failure to connect. As a normal object in any kitchen, here it is empty when thought to be full and full when thought to be empty. Later, Wesley starving and unaware that his mother has filled the fridge again, kills the maggot-ridden lamb in order to eat it. The lamb has become the sixth member of the family, an amusingly macabre travesty of a household pet. At the beginning of Act 3, Weston lovingly tells it the chilling story of a giant eagle preying on the discarded testicles of castrated lambs. But its bloody slaughter by Wesley reminds us animals are also killed here. Its unhealthy presence near the fridge reminds us of the close relationship between live flesh and processed meat, between the raw and the cooked. The farming family are erratic producers of the former and erratic consumers of the latter. The play makes us all too aware of the organic relationship between the two, but somehow the family itself contrives never to learn the lesson.

Two instances of disrecognising tell us much about Shepard's theatre. The first is the incident of Emma talking to the fridge, the second that of Weston talking to the lamb. They show the strengths of the playwright's technique and the sheer flair for driving through hyped-up melodrama with total dramatic conviction. They display in equal measure his inventiveness and tendency to excess. In the first incident mentioned above where Emma talks to the empty fridge, she is being watched without her knowledge by Taylor, the crooked lawyer who is having an affair with her mother and setting up the deal to get the family's land. Her treating of the refrigerator as if it were human is clearly absurd. But because it is animistic it is also extremely funny. The fridge is treated in turn as a confidante, a tiny baby and a brazen cheat. 'You don't have to be ashamed,' Emma commiserates, 'I've had worse. I've had worse. I've had to take my lunch to school wrapped in a Weber's bread wrapper.' And then: 'You'll get some little eggs tucked into your sides and some yellow margarine tucked into your little drawers...'[2] The object has become a helpless, adorable child to be cooed over. But the mood changes just as quickly as Emma promises it frozen chicken and then remembers the fate of the chicken she had cut up and left in the fridge. The mute object is greeted – 'You Motherfucker!' – in mid-sentence with an unexpected curse.

The reason for this is already clear to the audience. At the beginning of the act, Emma has found out that her mother has boiled the chicken she had prepared for a cookery class at school. To add insult to injury the contemptuous Wesley has urinated all over her chicken charts where they still lie on the kitchen floor. As the fifth member of the family, the fridge takes the blame for the selfish actions of two of the others. The attribution of blame is common in domestic drama, but here Shepard turns it into a brilliant comic device. If Emma can talk lovingly to a kitchen appliance because it can neither understand or talk back, she can blame things on it for the same reason. Yet, as we have suggested, the fridge is also a kind of totemic object seen as having the power to produce the miracle of food, a halfway house between the raw and the cooked. Shepard makes it a central metonym in the tradition of Gabler's pistols, Treplev's seagull and Lenny's cheese sandwich. If Vladimir's carrot might just as well be a turnip, the fridge, however, cannot be anything but a fridge. There are limits to disrecognising. It cannot be mistaken for a cooker or a washing-machine. With affection and cunning, Shepard elevates the constant action of opening and shutting it to the realm of destiny. It is quintessential tragicomic fate, empty when it is meant to be full, full when it is thought to be empty. Things not worth eating, like Weston's desert artichokes are lovingly put into it while things taken out of it, like Emma's chicken, are taken out for the wrong purpose. Fate-as-nutrition in any household is usually determined by who puts what in the fridge and when. But it is never viewed that way here. For each of the family in turn, opening the fridge becomes a search for the miracle of plenty, as if sumptuous food might have been put there by an unseen hand. None of the family, however, manages to connect the act of putting food in the fridge with the act of opening the fridge to find food in it. Nobody knows who has put what in or when. Chaos and solipsism produce the illusion of fate. Such fate is Shepard's comic travesty of the American dream in the age of mass consumption. 'We're not part of the starving class!' Emma insists, but for all the food which is in their fridge they might just as well be.

Emma's talking to the fridge is play-ful in nature, and takes play to the point of complete eccentricity. Shepard makes this clear by having the lawyer silently witness the act, too obviously filtering the gaze of the audience. It works as a kind of escape-clause one never finds in Beckett. But Emma's talk is a vital kind of inventiveness, a vivid form of extemporising, and not really eccentric at all. Her seeing the fridge as something other than what it is, is a form of disrecognising, of playful misidentification. So, more conventionally, is Taylor's gaze from the doorway. The 'play' becomes serious when she remembers the fate of her chicken. Yet it remains play. In conventional melodrama she would have to shout the word 'Mother!' and clench her fists in fury. Instead she calls the fridge a motherfucker. The choice of the epithet is not altogether arbitrary as her mother's lover is standing in the doorway and is the person with whom she comes face to face as she turns round.

The second incident, soon after, illustrates the importance of repetition in tragicomedy. We can recall the way that *Godot* simultaneously repeats and changes the events of Act 1 in Act 2. Here the father repeats the daughter's assault on the fridge but with a difference. First of all he has to contend with the sick lamb Wesley has brought into the warm of the kitchen. As Weston finally confronts the fridge, Shepard again uses the device of the unseen bystander. This time it is Wesley who looks on as his father rants and raves, as he speaks to the lamb and the fridge then shouts at the house in general. By the use of large capitals in the text for Weston's tantrum, Shepard knowingly mocks the melodrama he creates. And the scene also needs the challenge of Wesley at the end – 'What you're yelling for? There's nobody here.'[3] – to deflate Weston's histrionic rage. But the key source of humour is the encounter with the lamb:[4]

> WESTON: (*to lamb*): What in hell are you doin' in here? (*He looks around the space, to himself*) Is this inside or outside? This is inside, right. This is the inside of the house. Even with the door out it's still the inside. (*to lamb*) So what the hell are you doing in here if this is the inside?

Weston literally does not know where he is. The kitchen has no door because he has kicked it down in a drunken fit the previous night and cannot remember doing it. The lamb is on the inside when it should be on the outside and Weston demands of the mute animal that it rescue him from his confusion. This double lack of recognition ironises a central convention of the naturalist stage. The three-walled room assumes an inside and an outside. It also assumes one can be distinguished from the other. The dramatic suspense of Pinter, as noted, comes from the unexpected opening and closing of doors. Here there is no door to open or close. It has been battered down the previous night, and Weston is responsible for his own bafflement. The lamb completes the bewildering picture. Seeing the poor animal, he thinks for a moment he is leaving the house when he is in fact entering it. As near-hallucination, disrecognising fazes him out. This is just more than play on stage convention. It plays just as much on the domestic convention of entering one's own home as the most familiar of places. The family home, like the family itself, has become unfamiliar. The detailed stage directions give a further clue. Weston, family head and self-styled provider, is dressed like a drunken tramp, a passing vagrant who has spotted an empty door-frame. Even the homecoming of the prodigal father is disguised by appearance. Returning home and entering his kitchen, he looks like a homeless person. Appearances complement his failure to recognise his own kitchen. His subsequent complaint – that he is 'MR SLAVE LABOUR COME HOME TO REPLENISH THE LARDER' – establishes him in his normal role, but does so by showing him as travesty of that role. If this is the ritual return of the male breadwinner to feed his starving family, no one wants to eat his dubious produce.

Weston is typical of the weak, collapsing patriarchs of tragicomedy, the grotesque buffoons of Genet or Soyinka trapped by popular uprising, or Beckett's anti-heroes trapped by disability. They are enmeshed in a game whose moves they cannot control. While Hamm and Pozzo thunder despairingly at an unrecognisable world, Shepard domesticates the convention of impotence. The 'breadwinner' enters his own home, which is in the process of being sold behind his back, and has no discernible impact. When he starts shrieking, nobody is listening, not even Wesley who can hear him. Shepard thus undermines the coexistence of entrance and presence which is so crucial for naturalist drama. Weston makes his entrance in a comic void. The only other object to greet him is the lamb in the pen, but that 'meeting' is somewhat arbitrary. Using animals in stage production is risky enough because they are so unpredictable. But perhaps that is what Shepard had in mind. In the one production of the play, the lamb – played by a full grown ewe – rushed to greet Weston as he entered the kitchen, but when he started shrieking, took no notice of him at all.

The monologues of Emma and Weston are both comic examples of Shepardian obsession. His characters are not moral beings unbaring their souls, but characters who perform like deranged actors. The obsessive monologue does not wait upon its audience. Impulsive and often desperate, it is acted out as if an animal or household object is equivalent to human presence. We have more than an echo here of that unseen presence, narcotics, which resonates through Shepard's work. We are once more in the arena of psychic wipe-outs, trance, paranoia and phobic obsession. Shepard merely contrives to make them more homely and familiar. But the story Wesley tells his mother at the end, the parable about the eagle and the tom cat he has inherited from his father, reasserts the primal horror of the American home. The eagle swoops down on his prey but in mid-air the tomcat fights back. The eagle then tries to free himself but the tomcat refuses to let go, knowing that if he does, he will fall. It is a graphic cartoon of destructive clinging which brings down the victimiser and victim. As Ella concludes, 'Both of them come crashing down. Like one whole thing.'[5]

Shepard works within a national tradition of melodrama which overwhelms and simplifies, which gives us full-blown feeling rather than its fine tuning, which strives for instantaneous effect rather than moral complexity. But he harnesses that melodrama to modernist ends. Excessive self-expression – an American curse – becomes an instrument of shock. He also overturns the optimistic and idealising strain in melodrama. His characters are not only victims of evil conspiracy. They are equally victims of their own confusion, their failures to perceive. Too diminished ever to attain a recognition of their fallen circumstance, they remain unwitting victims. Emma's sudden change of voice as she talks to the fridge, the switch from cloying concern to abuse, is a typical switch of posture. It mirrors the pattern of her general switch in the play from high-school girl concerned with her cookery class to rampaging juvie, a juvenile delinquent who glowingly chooses a life of crime. The shock of course is that we expect this from the male, not the female, the brother, not the sister. Yet her escape from the collapsing family is not a noble release into a better world, as it might be with a traditional heroine. Shepard mocks that tradition by making her trade one doomed, impossible world for another.

His dramatic imagination shows naturalist virtues which have often been maligned. If his family is a farming family then the placing of the lamb in a sheep-pen in the kitchen lets us know it. The macabre humour links the production of food to its haphazard consumption. We see the maggot-ridden lamb too close to the fridge for comfort and our ideas of hygiene are accordingly tested – though it is not something which bothers Wesley or Weston. We notice what they ignore. Yet propinquity of beast and object also insinuates in our mind the fact that one could be destined for the other. The fridge is where the lamb could end up after being slaughtered and in sheltering it from the cold, Wesley has merely brought it nearer to its doom. Later when he kills the lamb to eat it, he does so because he mistakenly thinks there is no food in the fridge. He cannot imagine his mother would fill it with groceries or that his father would be using them to cook breakfast. Misunderstanding leads to ritual sacrifice. The slaughter of the innocent animal complements the start of Emma's menstruation and the dressing up of Wesley in the old clothes his father has discarded in the garbage can. The latter are classic portents of doom. But they are also founded in the everyday world. This constant play on the ordinary challenges our sense of the ordinary and lays bare the various devices of its dramatic staging. They are a tribute to the triumph of Shepard's dramatic form.

While *Curse of the Starving Class* displays a tragic inevitability in the collapse of the family, *Buried Child* does the opposite. It shows tragic inevitability in the unlikely continuation of the family inheritance. In the unlikely rescue of the family line by the returning grandson, it has obvious similarities with *The Homecoming*. But its shock ending is, in one sense, more conventional than Pinter's. It is the male who takes over the household while his outraged girlfriend leaves him to it. It is not female absence so much as the blood kinship of males which fascinates Shepard, the trap of genealogy rather than the absent mother. The 'homecoming' is the other fate of the peripatetic American male, the drifter, the transient, the self-uprooted, to be repeated rather differently in

True West. Yet Shepard is also satirising the famous 'homecoming' enshrined by Norman Rockwell, the sacrosanct American Family of the rural hinterland which tearfully recognises the return of its own. Here the difference with Pinter is much greater. Shepard is brutally challenging a cherished national myth in an age where the myth itself is looking more ragged than ever. The power of his shock effects is as great here as it has ever been. By the end, when Vince claims his inheritance after his grandfather's death, he has accepted a desolation beyond civilisation, modernity, the future, beyond any sense of what an audience will understand by those terms.

Shepard's Illinois farming family is both caricature and tragic presence. His characters are all travesties of 'real' people of the land, 'real' farmers, of their historical ancestors with their sturdy frontier spirit. They are desiccated, down-at-heel and demoralised. Unlike the alfalfa farm in *Curse* one feels their land is too remote and isolated for commercial predation. They have, it seems, been left to rot. They are forgotten people and only the 'homecoming' of Vince and Shelley brings external judgement upon them. Here with a neat irony Shepard makes his young shiftless brats into the guardians of our common sense. They share and mediate our sense of the madness of life down on the farm. At a deeper level in the work, play is structured into aggro-effects more reminiscent of Bond than the anguished extemporising in the early Beckett. More important than inventiveness of response, than the power of word-play which at times degenerates into mere harangue, is the sudden and unexpected act. The gestic act defines a moment, a character, a relationship in a way that is powerfully uncanny. It is a sudden gesture which lies at the very borders of reason, but is not, therefore, irrational. Shepard is powerfully adept at giving us the uncanny mismatch of emotion and reason, of feeling and intention, in a single and complete gesture.

The gesture here is both play-ful and serious. At one level it is too childlike to be tragic. At another it is too emotionally powerful and inexplicable not to be. By combining alienation and aggro-effects, Shepard distances us from his characters yet makes us respond to them emotionally at the same time. We see this in the very first scene where Dodge is watching a flickering soundless television screen while the unseen Hailie, his wife, shouts at him from upstairs. Tilden, the elder, middle-aged son enters, wearing ill-fitting work-clothes. He is 'burnt-out and displaced'. His arms are laden with fresh ears of corn. Dodge immediately accuses him of stealing it since corn, he claims, has not grown at the back of the house since 1935. The corn is a deranged miracle which seems to make nonsense of normal history, and Tilden reveres it in child-like wonder. As he begins to husk it, he does so like a boy at play, and when his parents accuse him of stealing he weeps like an overgrown child. The simple gestures of the bringing and husking of the corn combine natural wonder and childish regression. For the audience there is a genuine horror embedded in Tilden's impossible innocence, as if they see on stage the cruellest possible travesty of one of their strongest yearnings.

There are further shock-effects. When Dodge talks himself to sleep on the sofa with his whisky bottle, Tilden lovingly covers his body with husks of corn. After Tilden has gone, Bradley, his younger brother, enters to cut his father's hair with electric clippers. As the first act ends we see him violently knock away Dodge's baseball cap and the husks of corn covering Dodge's face. As the second act begins, Bradley has gone but as Vince and Shelley enter the house, we see Dodge still sleeping on the sofa, his head cut and bleeding as if he had been half scalped. As in Beckett the central sequence is repeated in the next act. Once again the idiocy of Tilden is followed by the cruelty of Bradley. Tilden comes in to confront Vince and Shelley, cradling carrots in his arms just as he had previously cradled corn. In a reflex act of domesticity Shelley is persuaded to take them from his arms and peel them. It is a parody of the sexual division of labour one might expect down on the farm. The man gathers and the woman prepares. But the infantile idiocy of Tilden's gesture which appears to be without conscious purpose is made into a chilling dramatic sequence. As in the first act idiocy is followed by violation. The disabled Bradley with over-muscular torso hobbles in on his wooden leg after his brother has left. At their first encounter, he forces Shelley to open her mouth and penetrates it with his finger in an act of symbolic rape, an assault which closes the second act when he goes to stand over the sleeping Dodge, covering his father's face with his coat. As his hands remain still in the position of holding the coat, he turns to Shelley and smiles.

In the final act fortunes are reversed when Shelley kidnaps Bradley's wooden leg and leaves him threshing helplessly on the sofa. Bradley is seen to be as impotent as his brother is idiotic. Dodge, the dying patriarch, is flanked by inept, incompetent sons who present no challenge to his lame authority. But the playful gestures of anguished dementia the two brothers make would not of themselves sustain the dramatic action of the play. They serve as a counterpoint to the forms of disrecognising which equally define its structure. These start on a low key with the mocking and disbelieving Shelley who cannot imagine life on the farm to be what it is, but then strike a more disconcerting note as Vince fails to gain habitual recognition from Dodge as his grandson or from Tilden as his son. At first it seems that six years' absence is too much for their dim memory. But Shepard makes it clear that neither of his diminished fathers has any capacity for making links with the past, for acknowledging its return in any form. As Vince bends his thumb behind his knuckles and drums his teeth with his fingers to try and provoke memories of his past presence at the family dinner table, nothing registers. If the two fathers are the key to family lineage, to the linking of past and present, to the identity which operates through patriarchy, then all of those things have broken down. In practice, they cannot recognise family resemblances.

The tragic farce is compounded further by Dodge's other failures. He tells Shelley his ancestry is 'a long line of corpses!' For him, the past 'never happened'. Shelley finds that he will not identify pictures hanging up on the bedroom wall of himself as a young man, or of the young woman with red hair, or the child she is holding in her arms, looking down at it 'like it was somebody else's.'[6] But the failure is in part wilful, for the child is the skeleton in the family's cupboard. Veiled references to it throughout fail to add up to a clear picture of its origin or its parentage. But Shelley has planted the seed in Dodge's mind of a kind of memory. His subsequent chronicle of the unwanted child in the family recalls Hamm's chronicle of the child in *Endgame*. The audience must wonder if, in some form, it is still 'there', in the household. In Dodge's version, it is the child Hailie has given birth to in middle age when they already have grown sons and when they have failed to sleep in the same bed for six years. In the same version, it is Tilden who has taken the child to his heart, as if it were his own. Here Shepard's timing has a distinct melodramatic pathos. As they speak of the forgotten child, Tilden's real son, now grown and completely drunken, reappears at the screen door, smashing bottles against the wall.

In typical fashion Shepard mixes modernist ambiguity and

dramatic mayhem. We never know the true story of the child and one of the reasons is the chaos of conflicting actions which fly through the last act. Shelley steals Bradley's leg, Vince smashes broken bottles against the porch and uses a knife to cut up the door screen while Hailie exhorts her ineffectual priest to prevent pandemonium. Here Shepard is carried away by his own excess. Dodge's last will and testament, his sudden unnoticed death and Vince's unlikely assumption of his inheritance as Shelley flees, mock the denouement of popular melodrama but cannot escape it. It requires something else, something more chilling to overcome its predilection for chaos. In the final dramatic gest, Shepard rescues and redeems the play with an ultimate revelation. Tilden enters, cradling in his arms the muddied corpse of a buried child. It seems to be the child of middle age Hailie has rejected. But Tilden's cherishing of it takes on a more chilling and poignant meaning. Though we shall never know for sure, it seems to be the misbegotten fruit of an Oedipal union between mother and son. Vince's father cradles it with the same fond idiocy that he had previously cradled the corn and the carrots. The corpse now has that same vegetable quality, looking for all the world like an armful of dead crop. It is akin to the corpse in the second section of Eliot's *The Waste Land* which sprouts back up through the earth from whence it has come. It can also be seen as Vince's dead brother, or a version of Vince himself. As Vince reclines on the sofa, in exactly the same posture as his deceased grandfather, now lying on the floor, the other 'homecoming' unexpectedly takes place, the entry of the long deceased 'brother/uncle'. The corpse is Vince's alter ego, his dead shadow, whose appearance stresses that the unlikely inheritance is not the rescuing of the family line, but part of the genealogy of death.

When Vince dons the mantle of family inheritance, he cloaks himself in a living death. He is as dead as the buried child is 'alive' to his father. And we also have a further possibility, that Vince himself is the child in Hailie's picture. For Vince's 'absent mother' is never explained. At no point does he, or anyone else, even mention her. The various refusals to recognise may therefore work on two planes, the first the obvious one of rural idiocy, but the second the evasion of an awful truth no one wishes to contemplate. If it is possible Tilden is the father of the buried child, it is equally possible that Vince is the real child of middle age for Dodge and Hailie and that Tilden, posing as Vince's father, is an older brother. Thus Vince can be seen as the uncle or the brother *or* the uncle/brother of the buried child. Hailie – whom he spontaneously calls 'grandma' – would then be his unacknowledged mother. Who, one might indeed ask, is the real 'buried child'? The play's subtext, whose sense of the uncanny dissolves most of the over-wrought melodrama, reverberates with unanswered questions. Disrecognising may be the malaise of an ingrown and isolated rural existence. It may on the other hand be a calculated evasion of another kind of ingrown existence – incest. As tragicomedy the play moves between the two, between opposite ends of its structure of feeling, between hilarity and horror, between a com-edy of errors and tragic desperation.

The experience of the play defies any schematic solution. As in *Endgame* we have the experience of interpretations floating on a sea of uncertainty. Re-reading the play offers different meanings. Specific exchanges can take on a different hue. When Dodge refuses Vince's title of 'grandpa' it could be just a crotchety rejection of the family line. But equally it could be that Vince is *his* son or that Tilden is *not* his son. Such speculation might be called idle since it challenges the explicit stage directions Shepard gives us, the fixing of the relationship of Dodge to Tilden and Tilden to Vince. Yet the play itself does not fix them, and in many instances the dialogue contradicts them. The flux of disrecognising encour-ages the deconstructing of relationships. It sets in motion an urge to detect a truth which, as in *Endgame*, is always elusive and never final. We discover a secret buried child, but never *its* secret. The family as the most familiar of entities is also a repository of secrets it does not wish to reveal, even to its own kind. Supposed to provide the fix of certain genealogy in a fraught world, it turns out to be even more uncertain than the world beyond kin, the hostile, impersonal world 'out there'.

In the last scene the twin corpses of youth and age, child and old man, flanking the unlikely inheritor, signify the spiritual death of his inheritance. Vince may have displaced his burnt-out father and his disabled uncle but they will live on to plague him. He has lost his girl and inherited a mausoleum. As Tilden cradles the corpse of the child, Hailie's voice echoes from afar the miracle of rain and new crops in a changed land. Like Oswald's final despairing plea in *Ghosts* she invokes the miracle of the sun. But the play's tragic victims have burnt themselves out and failed to learn from the mistakes of others. The inheritance fails to bring forth knowledge.

Recognition and catharsis, the pattern of Oedipus and all great tragedy, is replaced here by catharsis without recognition. Vince openly embraces a dead circle of repetition and turns it to a refrain of hope and joy, living on in blissful ignorance. It is the antithesis of a tragic heroism which finds meaning on the point of death and destruction. Like Shepard's other heroes, Vince survives as an active victim, conspiring in the trap which shackles him, not even realising he has forfeited freedom. Shelley's flight proves that freedom still exists, but only for those outside the family. For those within, existence is a tyranny which continually repeats itself. It is a tyranny none can bring themselves to acknowledge. The comic farce of the family's endless convolutions ends in tragic and petrified darkness. They are manic yet helpless.

The buried child echoes the living child of Hamm's chronicle in *Endgame*. The field of corn, the 'miracle' that Hailie claims to see out of the window, echoes Hamm's story of his encouragement to the painter, his evocation outside the asylum of the 'rising corn' and the 'sails of the herring fleet'. But for Hamm this is a distant memory of the good old days before the greyness of the zero world which Clov now claims to see from the tiny windows. The thread of optimism in Shepard to some extent inverts Beckett, for it ends the play on a high note – even though the vision is possibly nothing more than hallucination or fantasy. We no more know if Hailie is giving us an objective picture of the world outside the farmhouse than if Clov is giving us one of the world outside Hamm's bunker. In Shepard there is always a residue of hope to be set against the darkest fate and this makes him a distinctive American writer, one who is never part of the nullity of European apocalypse. In *Buried Child* hope and catastrophe live side by side. The mood oscillates from manic humour to tragic horror and back again. But hope is never extinguished.

Shepard III: Re-Enacting the Myth of Origin

Compared with his family drama, Shepard's two subsequent plays, *True West* and *Fool for Love*, can be seen as chamber pieces. They pare down and strip away the ballast of the madcap family intrigue. What they lose in scope and power they gain through a concentrated purity of acting and re-enacting the puzzle of origin. They are in effect covert family dramas where the larger family is absent, and the relationship is that of siblings in *True West* or lovers in *Fool for Love*. In the latter it could well be both. But origin entails place as well as kin, myth as well as ancestry. Who Shepard's heroes actually are now depends on where they come from in a wider sense, where they were born as well as who they were born to. The nature of the places in which they have lived can no more be taken for granted than their ancestors. Though they differ significantly in terms of place both plays evoke the desert in Southern California, a locale which for Shepard refuses any obvious pigeonholing. The suburban home of Lee and Austin's mother forty miles east of Los Angeles in *True West*, and May's bleak motel room on the fringe of the Mojave in *Fool for Love* are both just on this side of civilisation, nearing the edge of a sparsely populated wilderness. In both plays we are witnessing an enclosed action on the verge of something bleak and vast, something which makes the identity of the modern West just as problematic as the mythical 'true west' which preceded it. Moreover, one cannot be understood without the other.

Shepard's approach to the 'west' here differs radically from his earlier fantasy pieces and also Arthur Kopit's freewheeling ludic spectacle *Indians*. In its techniques and staging, Kopit's play is at an extreme tangent to Shepard's later work, yet it shares some important affinities. In his study of the strange relationship between Buffalo Bill Cody and the Sioux leader, Sitting Bull, Kopit is particularly fascinated by one important dimension in the exploitation of the American Indian. Cody's famous Wild West Show *preceded* the final disintegration of Sitting Bull's tribe and the tragic slaughter of their chief. His play appeared in the late sixties at a period of the critical examination of American legend, of disenchantment with the cheap myths of the Hollywood Western and renewed concern with the historical plight of the Indians and the acquisition of their land. For Kopit, Cody and Sitting Bull both become commodified figures of popular spectacle before the actual historical fate of the Indian has been decided. Here myth is *not* a retrospective imposition upon a history which has run its course. Myth itself is history in the making. The Wild West Show is as much a part of American history as the battle at Little Big Horn. Buffalo Bill, the legend manufactured with the aid of the dime novelist, Ned Buntline, is as much a part of history as William Cody.

In a particularly amusing scene in the play – which links the politics of theatricality to the theatricality of politics – Buffalo Bill's team of Western troupers lose their souls to their stage personas in a performance for the President and the First Lady. Kopit is aware of the theatrical nature of politics in his own epoch, and his play is to some extent anachronistic. It reads back into the nineteenth century the performative culture of the electronic age. The special audience in the White House ballroom welcome the performers onstage as kindred spirits. The Indians are played by Germans or Italians from Brooklyn while Cody, Hickok and the rest become travesties of themselves. They are like Shepard's rock stars but in an earlier epoch, frozen in their own image, here taking their cues from Buntline who prompts them from offstage. When Hickok, tired of having to play himself onstage, breaks the frame by stabbing Buntline and trying to make off with the Indian squaw, he merely draws even more rapturous applause from the First Lady. Kopit's style is that of a self-conscious melodramatic exaggeration. But it works. Cody and Hickock have boxed themselves into a corner. The performance of self has become a trap.

Kopit juxtaposes the theatrical shenanigans of the Wild West Show to the political inveigling over treaties between the government and the Sioux Indians, which ends in the murder of Sitting Bull. There is a real history, perhaps too solemn and formal in its treatment here, which runs parallel to the circus of games. In the end Cody is unable to control either. The most telling moment in the play occurs towards the end when Hickok, now a fully-fledged cultural hustler offers the scared and conscience-stricken Cody no support for the plight of the Sioux but instead a new recipe for fame. It is 'simultaneous presence'. A group of Buffalo Bills enters with the same florid buckskins as Cody, all wearing Cody masks. Hickok wishes to export the image all over the American continent. 'We could go on like this', Hickok exclaims, *'forever!'*[1] Cody tries to blast his stand-ins out of existence. They fall, rise again and disappear. In the age of cinema, which the scene prefigures, he would be even more helpless to prevent the perpetual presentation of his own image in which his diminishing self has been buried alive. The affliction is Cody's tragicomic horror, the moment where organised farce comes back to plunge him into perpetual torment.

Like Hoss, Cody is tormented by the mythic self which has run out of control at the very moment when the vestiges of the authentic self seem to have vanished. Lee in *True West* and Eddie in *Fool for Love* are contemporary versions, and very different ones, of the same mythic predicament. They are so at several stages removed. Kopit uses a real historical figure as a mythic embodiment of a mythical predicament. In his muddling failure to prevent the oppression of the Indians and the seizure of their lands he is a humanitarian version of the failed patriarch of tragicomedy. But Lee and Eddie are nobodies in the inheritance stakes of the true west, marginal drifters, unlikely hangers-on, impossible imitations of celebrity. They are, however, more powerful creations than the more obvious cowboys of Shepard's middle period, the captured cowboy rock star of *Cowboy Mouth*, the unlikely Wyoming saviours at the end of *Geography of a Horse Dreamer*, the mythic reincarnations of *The Unseen Hand* or *The Holy Ghostly*. One must also add that the Eddie in the dramatic text of *Fool for Love* is far more compelling than Shepard's screen performance of his hero in the version he scripted for Robert Altman. Altman's flawed film makes us only too aware of the implosive power of the play's naturalistic space, and equally of Shepard's failure to be a good movie actor.

For Kopit the commodification of Cody's image as a major celebrity is vital to the establishment of Western myth. By contrast, Lee and Eddie are desperately thrashing life out of that myth in its age of decline. They are literally flogging a dead horse. As modern men of the West they have few mythical qualities, nor can they renew the myth which others have forged. Yet *True West* and *Fool for Love* are vitally important works because they have such a strong and enduring sense of contemporary America. They also highlight a central relationship which brings the later Shepard closer to Beckett and Pinter and shows equally his indebtedness to the early Albee. If Lee and Austin have echoes of Didi and Gogo and of the brothers in *The Caretaker*, their power-plays are in a direct line of descent from the encounter of Jerry and Peter in *The Zoo Story*. Shepard's work is an advance and an inversion of earlier forms of American tragicomedy. The community of junkies openly waiting for their fix in Jack Gelber's *The Connection* becomes an anti-community in *The Tooth of Crime* or *Action*. Likewise, the separation of roles in *The Zoo Story*, active and passive, hip and square, embittered drifter and respectable publisher, is an important charge for the dramatic momentum of Shepard's work. But the latter fails to maintain those absolute separations. Its key is transfer and reversal. In *True West* Lee and Austin trade roles in true Shepardian fashion but also draw attention to that other feature of his work. In the constant movement from the outside to the inside or vice versa, they also swap personalities. 'Personality' here is a fixed point of departure, but no more. For it is also self-invented, negotiable, pliable to the point of nonentity. The clash of opposites thus turns into the transfer of opposites. Mobility produces the hustler. Failure produces cheap nemesis.

True West shows us that there are two kinds of hustling, the conventional and the outrageous. Lee and Austin are two versions of the split American persona brought up on the myth of the American Dream. In a secondary light, they could be seen as conflicting aspects of Shepard himself. The opening scene is superbly tense and beautifully written. It shows the invasion of the brother-outsider into the suburban home of the absent mother, where Austin, the good scriptwriter, is dutifully plying his trade.

The tension is due not just to fear of the unpredictable intruder but also to the fragile dividing-line between compliance and total disregard for the order of things. In the uncanny sense of doubling which Shepard sets up between the brothers, it is as if Austin knows from the start the threat that his brother brings. That threat is not just a challenge to the normal way of doing things but the knife-edge alternative which one senses Austin has repressed in order to engage business-as-usual. Lee is one version of the true adventurer Austin merely writes about in his subordinate role within the Hollywood dream-trade. At the same time Lee is a dissolute freelance tramp from the desert, the bane of any sense of wholesome adventure, an affront to true macho heroism. Shepard's clinical dissection of the underbelly of the American Dream in the post-Vietnam era evokes comparison with the doubling effects in the fiction of Robert Stone. Lee and Austin have that close, symbiotic relationship of John Converse and Greg Hicks in *Dog Soldiers* or of Holliwell and Pablo Tresor in *A Flag for Sunrise*. They are incestuous combatants who mirror each other even at the extremes of hostility, the one literate and knowledgeable, the other marginal and desperate.

In contemporary America the fragile fabric of the social order strives to contain both these extremes and provide them with a common sense of purpose. It seldom does. Yet that same fragile consensus relies on their difference, their separation, the rejection by the literate and the knowledgeable of personal and social extremes, their sane refusal of the demons of danger. In Stone and Shepard that separation is never maintained. The crossing of the boundary at the end of *Zoo Story* where Jerry deliberately impales himself on the knife in Peter's hand, has begun much earlier here. Unlike Peter, Austin in *True West* lacks resilience. His attachment to the conventions of his profession are made to appear skin-deep once Lee has persuaded Saul Kimmer, Austin's producer, to contract his story instead. The golf-match between Lee and Saul at Saul's country-club looks far-fetched on the printed page. But John Malkovich, in his stunning portrayal of Lee for the Steppenwolf production of the play, brought out brilliantly the subtext of bisexual hustling, that last fateful step in the play of male bonding which Austin, the married man with kids, could never take. Austin goes drunk and beserk, not out of peak, but because his strategy of playing the game has been shown, by his brother of all people, to be worthless. Though he has been totally correct and obeyed the rules of the game, he has never internalised them.

It is not that Lee and Austin trade personalities in the psychological sense. Rather, they swap trajectories. It is not so much that each tries to take on the role of the other but that each tries to take the path which is preordained for the other. The results are both comic and tragic. In the scene where Lee is attacking the typewriter with a nine-iron and Austin is arraying his set of stolen toasters for a mammoth breakfast, Shepard orchestrates a harmonious pandemonium. The unease that each has for the other's trade becomes visceral in the extreme. Austin steals a clutch of the most valueless objects in the neighbourhood family kitchens while Lee demolishes the typewriter because the ribbon is constantly sticking, and because it cannot produce in words the images he has in his head. As elsewhere the most graphic action has a cartoon quality of Freudian regression. The toast seems to pop up in unison with each downward stroke of the nine-iron. When their mother unexpectedly returns to survey her ransacked home the two men are suddenly like little boys left alone in the house too long, whose 'play' has got out of hand.

The unsystematic destruction of the house proceeds both through neglect – failing to water the plants – but equally through a sense of grim purpose. Lee pulls out the phone not for kicks but because he cannot get the number of the woman he wants in Bakersfield. The drunken brothers destroy the kitchen not as deranged lunatics but as incompetent demolition men. Here Shepard joins the Brechtian exposure of the stage as artifact to the blank disrecognition of the returning mother. More important he fuses it to the brittleness of the sense of place. It is not just the destruction of the bourgeois suburban home which is at issue. It is also the call of the wild, like the howl of the coyotes from the hills which lures the local cocker-spaniels to their deaths. The naturalist stage is as fragile here as the suburban home whose interior it portrays. The home is too near to the desert for its own good. The set is destroyed because of the vulnerable setting. It is this elective affinity of the inside and the outside which makes the denouement of the play so compelling. We sense that Austin's desire to go into the desert with his brother has the same lure of danger to be found in the coyote's call to the spaniel. The rootless suburban home in Southern California cannot atone for its fragility by having all the latest domestic comforts. In the stage directions for the final scene, Shepard stresses not only the ravaged nature of a stage full of debris, but also the flooding of it by an intense yellow light which makes it look like 'a desert junkyard at high noon'. As the brothers sweat profusely over their mangled script, the coolness of the previous scenes has gone. An unseen hand, it appears, has turned off the air conditioning.

The regression to play and childhood, so destructive in adults, is mirrored in the return of civilisation back into desert. When their returning mother disturbs them, the brothers are in full flow, oblivious to their surroundings, trying to create for the movies their version of the myth of the 'true west'. In a sense, they are both trapped, locked into the mythical representation of the authentic West Lee desires to create on the printed page and the celluloid screen. But the words and the themes have been so worked over that they are all clichés. And the brothers are still at cross purposes. Lee is entranced by the mythical fix of the West he has lived through, Austin by the lure of the actual life his brother has lived. The crossover creates a stalemate to be resolved only through violence. But the attack by Austin on Lee, inverting the earlier fear that Austin has of being attacked, solves nothing. Their mother treats it as the horseplay of over-excited boys rather than a fight to the death. Her wish that they fight outside when the house is already a scrapheap has its own comic irony. For her, it is over-exuberant play, whose seriousness she fails to recognise. More importantly she does not recognise the results of their previous over-exuberant play, the wreck that is her own house.

Her return confounds all American assumptions of 'home as found'. Home is wrecked. She fails to recognise it, and leaves. But her comic appearance, and confounding of all conventions of 'motherhood', is topped by her notorious assertion that 'Picasso's in town.' The humour comes not only because Picasso is dead and Southern California is, anyway, the last place one would expect to see him even when alive. 'Picasso' is, subliminally, a throw-away version of celebrity towards which her two sons are aspiring and which they will never attain. They will remain unknowns, for their haphazard trading in myth will never give them a public name. Their names indeed will never be named by someone totally ignorant of what they have actually done, as their mother is of Picasso. His name, however, does serve once more to remind us of the difference between the two brothers. Austin knows of him and knows he is dead. Lee has never heard of him. Yet mother insists on them accompanying her to see the great man in the local museum. Her chasing of celebrity mocks and echoes theirs. In the end Lee can give up on his 'dumb story' about 'two lamebrains chasin' each other across Texas' and head back for the desert alone. But Austin is in no man's land, wanting both the story and the great adventure, and ending up with neither.

The parable of Christ-like crucifixion which Albee dramatises in *The Zoo Story* is inappropriate here. Because the two brothers trade roles, one cannot end up, suddenly and dramatically, as the crucifier and the other as the crucified. If Austin had actually strangled Lee with the telephone cord, the ending would be unconvincing. For the two brothers have taken equal turns at being victimiser and victim. The absence of violent death, though not of destruction, at the end of Shepard's plays is a decisive turn from the temptations of melodrama. Such death often threatens but never finally comes. For a violent culture where murder is often arbitrary, as it is in contemporary America, to reproduce it on stage would be to risk the danger of caprice. There is a price to pay for avoiding cheap imitations of a dangerous life. The price here is that his ending offers no closure, that it is barely an ending at all. *True West* fakes an ending only to replace it with a stalemate. The two brothers, hostile, unreconciled, confront each other with no resolution of their fate.

The love relationships in *Fool for Love* and *A Lie of the Mind* represent a significant turn very late in Shepard's work to date. There is a vague prefiguring of the sex war in works like *Cowboy Mouth* and *La Turista* but really nothing much to go on. The new interest in heterosexual combat was, in a sense, overdue, and necessary if one is to make a full claim for Shepard's greatness. *Fool for Love*, in particular, is a vital work. To acclaim or reject it, though, purely for reasons of content would be short-sighted. Its form in general is a big advance, a landmark in Shepard's development as a playwright. Indeed the fate of the love affair cannot be separated from the changes that Shepard rings in the naturalist form, the many layerings and forms of 'double seeing' that make it realistic, Brechtian and hallucinatory all at the same time. The play is a single act with no separate scenes, straight and continuous. According to Shepard's stage directions the action should be 'relentless and without a break'. May's cheap motel room with its faded door, walls and bedspread is a masterpiece of natural observation, the perfect setting for a lover's quarrel of visceral intensity. Yet it is framed by the mysterious figure of the Old Man who sits down-stage in a rocking chair, on a raised platform outside of the stage and closer to the audience, commenting on the quarrels and the claims to truth. The relentless banter is blown up in taut expressionist fashion by the amplified sound of slamming doors as Eddie walks outside in disgust or May walks off into the bathroom in rage. The exits turn into entrances as they both always return to the sound of further slamming. Down-stage the Old Man will eventually leave his rocking chair and intrude on the action, thus breaking the naturalistic frame.

Penned in on all sides, Eddie and May occasionally leave the room but never the stage. They are always part of the action or adjacent to it until Eddie's final exit. It is quite appropriate that when Eddie leaves her for the Countess, May should pack and leave too. They are both there or neither is there, both present or both absent except for those brief moments.

When the play starts, Eddie, like Lee in *True West*, is already on-stage. When he leaves, May in turn leaves Martin, packing her suitcase and walking out. His exit is thus annulled by hers and Shepard dispenses with the melodrama of the deserted woman. After what has happened, neither wants to be left behind. Both have to go. In the world of motels and trailers, any one space is occupied only for a brief and finite time. There is no fight here for territorial possession, as there is in Pinter, to match the contest for personal possession. The fight for personal conquest seems to have no territory. It is everywhere and nowhere. The room, so vivid and immediate for the audience, belongs to neither of them. It is a nonentity. At the end, both want to forget it. To wreck it, as Lee and Austin wreck their mother's home, would have no point. The wrecking of motels cannot destroy illusions of domesticity. Instead, we know that each will go their separate way. The Brechtian device here is not the demolition of the fragile shell by its temporary occupants, but the vantage point outside it by the elusive character who is both a part of it and apart from it. The Old Man down-stage observes the couple much as the audience does. But he also has a fateful foreknowledge of them, talks to them and finally joins them on the stage. At the end, to complete the necessary circular movement, he moves slowly back to his platform after they have gone. He is both on the inside and the outside, part of us and part of them. Finally, though, his ghostly presence tells against him. A visitor from the past, a jointly hallucinated arbiter of fate with no power to arbitrate, he is marooned in no man's land. He is part real, part phantom.

The Brechtian effects work sporadically through the Old Man's breaking of the frame, through his unpredictable interventions or recollections. But they are undermined by the stronger proto-Nietzschean vision of truth as a form of the will-to-power. To the Brechtian concern with fable and the Nietzschean will-to-power we must add Shepard's continuing obsession with myth, the craving for rightful origin which here is the mother of invention. In Shepard, myth usually seduces his characters out of their depth and *Fool for Love* is no exception. To place themselves in terms of their genealogy, and what they aspire to, is to place themselves out of range of their own will. It is to confront them with the horror of their own helplessness, even if the myth is a lie. In a way this is O'Neill without the certainty of knowledge. Combating each other with conflicting interpretations of the truth, which each wants to impose on the other, and on the hapless Martin, the reluctant third party necessary for the whole imbroglio to unfold, each stands to gain only a Pyrrhic victory. To define themselves in history, in relation to their own 'father' who may or may not be the Old Man in the rocking chair, they make themselves equally the victims of history. Theirs is a Faustian quest with no demonic ending. Instead it becomes cyclical, repetitive, embittered, unresolved. It is insepar-able too from the trials of embittered passion. Indeed it is a sign of that passion, one of its addictive side-effects. Only through total exhaustion can things come to an end. At the end of exhaustion, though, when strength is restored, there is nothing to stop them beginning all over again. In *Fool for Love* mythical time is linear – a matter of lineage – but emotional time is purely cyclical. The lovers try to define who they are in terms of where they have come from, but their passion does not progress. It merely goes round and round, and at certain points on its orbit it appears to have disappeared because it is hidden from sight.

For Eddie and May, love and betrayal – the former being addicted to the latter – is a movable feast. The vast open spaces of the West are the traversing distances of escape and reconciliation. The points of intersection, the places where their paths cross, seem random. That illusion of freedom itself draws powerfully on Western myth. But the couple are fleeting rather than dominating figures of the landscape. As a stuntman heading into middle age and rivalled by the faster action of younger competitors, Eddie is at best an expert impersonator, a travesty of the Western hero. As someone who is paid to 'stand in' occasionally for leading actors who play real Western heroes, he is also a travesty of a travesty, a confederate in the process of double impersonation in the dying genre of the American Western. His haphazard profession there-fore puts him at two stages removed from historical reality while his wages afford him the opportunity of being a latter-day cowboy with no ranch or land to supplement his truck and horse-trailer. Eddie lassoes steers and horses mainly in front of the camera. In real life he lassoes bedposts in a motel room. In some ways, he is no better than a performing seal. May, too, working as a makeshift cook in a desert diner seems little more than a travesty of the mythical saloon girl the hero Eddie impersonates might meet in an old studio Western. Their encounter contains about it a sense of *déjà vu* in its version of the travelling hero passing through and the seasoned female veteran of the sex wars marooned in the middle of nowhere. But this contemporary encounter is not the meeting of stars. It is the meeting of nonentities. Eddie and May are nobodies.

The tight enclosed space of their reunion is matched by their diminutive stature, diminutive, that is, in terms of myth and of their status in the world. But denying them any glamour, distancing himself from them through the device of the Old Man, Shepard is still on their side. They are still characters, not devices, and like Lee and Austin, more Stanislavkian in their construction than in the earlier plays. Shepard thus achieves a balance between their diminutive status and their emotional power. Their affair is a catalogue of comic impossibilities. We do not identify with them. The tragic possibility that they were both born to the same father draws us back rather than towards them. But the emotional anguish they generate is still a powerful source of attraction. Love and its betrayals, the neurotic compulsion to repeat a passion which has been a constant source of disillusion, the anguished search for identity out of a compromised past – Shepard makes all these universal through his attention to particular detail. The tangle into which this leads the couple works as a kind of violent situation comedy. But the trap which prevents the tangle ever being unravelled has an enveloping darkness which clouds their knock-about fate.

For both, the reunion is a version of the game as fate. Eddie turns up unannounced. May cannot bring herself to enforce her demand that he depart. He takes a chance on the reunion's success and it is part of her addiction that May cannot immediately dispatch him. They both play the game, leaving partly to chance the outcome of any one encounter. But previous experience has built into the game the probability that he will produce a fantasy of future togetherness only to two-time her the moment that she starts to believe in it. The dream of the trailer stuck in its own vegetable patch with a corral for the horses is for May just another 'dumb fantasy' she refuses this time to be 'suckered into'. The sense of past betrayal accumulates and lengthens the odds on success. The 'compulsion to repeat', to use Freud's term, becomes neurotic because the more time goes on, the more the odds are stacked against success. But Shepard drives beyond neurosis to a deeper anguish and an impossible heritage. The return to the psychic landscape of past failures is deeper than a love-affair governed by the game of male betrayal and female revenge. It is a primal horror of the ties that bind.

Here the escape, the desertion, the fantasies of togetherness and compulsive duplicity seem part of a deeper trap. Yet we do not know what that trap is. The big lumbering Martin, May's local date, is captive audience to two conflicting chronicles of origin, Eddie's story that he and May are half brother and sister born to different mothers and the same father. But in the end the stories partly coincide. Denying Eddie's story, May continues it with her own twist, a twist which confounds the Old Man. May's version is that her mother has committed suicide after following the Old Man to Eddie's house. The Old Man pleads for Eddie to give the male version of events, but Eddie concurs with May's version. The stories are as true and false as the Old Man himself, who may exist, who may have existed in the lives of one or both of the couple, who may or may not be their father. On the blank wall of the motel room the Old Man claims to see the picture of Barbara Mandrell which he claims is his idea of realism. But there is no picture. The chronicles of the couple may have the same dubious status of the Old Man, who may have the status of the non-existent picture he claims to see. The play's dramatic tension tightens the grip of relativity. The truth about the past of Eddie and May seems no more knowable, no more certain, than the truth of the 'true west' of which they are descendants and travesties.

If they do not have the same father – and we shall never know – we feel by the end that they would need to invent him. What binds their passion in a world which appears to them so utterly random is incest. The compulsion to repeat has its source in blood as much as love. It is a homecoming as well as a return, though of course it has no home. The homecoming takes place anywhere, in rooms with which they have no affinity, in places that are just dots on the map. Family binds them, but only as remnants, as sole survivors. They have abandoned the family for the public world and for adult love, but standing Freud on his head they have brought the family with them by violating the very taboo that is meant to turn them outward. The ties that bind *them* are a wilful and painful travesty of the ties that bind. It is the Old Man who is forced to disrecognise their chronicle of the past. They know their own versions only too well, having been through them again and again, reinventing the past to make it scorch them with pain, to make it brand them with its mark in order to give the present meaning.

The dramatic device of the Old Man echoes the first appearance of Anna in that other memory-play, *Old Times*, where she seems at first to be a joint hallucination on the part of Kate and Deeley. By contrast, the Other Woman in Shepard's play never appears on-stage. The Countess is more of an apparition than the Old Man, a shadowy force of insane jealousy raining gunshots on the motel room in a fierce cameo of the revenger's tragicomedy. Yet the gunshots are real and we accept the couple's account of her black Mercedes as real in a way that we cannot accept the Old Man as real. On the other hand, the Old Man cannot be wished away as a hallucination. In a note on the characters in his stage directions, Shepard suggests the Old Man exists only in the minds of Eddie and May despite his physical presence. Yet he is much more than the ghost of Hamlet's father. The play has brought him to life. He indubitably *is*. But what he is we shall never know. Ambiguity attends him as the 'buried father' as it attends the muddied corpse of the 'buried child' in Shepard's earlier play of the same name. In both plays literal description in the stage directions is undermined by the ambiguities of a lineage which cannot be deciphered. Just as myth has to be given an origin, so origin has to be given a myth. We are trapped in a circle from which there is no way out.

There is no way out and therefore no catastrophic endings, and in tragicomedy there is no tragic death to create such ends. Tragicomedy is the genre of heroes who will not die, who will spring back to life as Lee springs out of the cord that Austin has tightened around his neck. Diminished they live and diminished they survive. Death has little it can take away from them that life has not already. They may have taken a tumble but not a fall. There is no absolute loss for themselves or for anyone else. They must survive, and their efforts to survive amuse us. If our laughter at times drowns the pain, we should not worry. That it is how it is meant to be. But the pain will go on. That, too, is how it is meant to be.

Notes

Chapter 1: Modernism and Tragicomedy

1. See *The Long Revolution* (Harmondsworth: Penguin, 1965), pp. 64–88; also *Marxism and Literature* (Oxford: Oxford University Press, 1977), pp. 128–35.
2. Peter Szondi, *Theory of the Modern Drama* (trans. Michael Hays) (Cambridge: Polity Press, 1987) p. 63.
3. *Just Play: Beckett's Theater* (Princeton: Princeton University Press, 1980), p. 13.
4. *Noten zur Literatur*, vol. 1 (Frankfurt: Suhrkampf, 1965), p. 54 ff.
5. See W. E. Haug, *Critique of Commodity Aesthetics: Appearance, Sexuality and Advertising in Capitalist Society* (trans. Robert Bock) (Cambridge: Polity Press, 1986), p. 57 f. For a study which advocates the postmodern embrace of performative culture and tries to find an inconoclastic role for the now-commodified subject, see Peter Sloterdijk, *Critique of Cynical Reason* (trans. Michael Eldred) (London: Verso, 1988). Drawing on Bakhtin, Sloterdijk puts forward carnivalisation as a conscious alternative to Adorno's 'melancholy science'.

Chapter 2: Play and Performative Culture

1. See Elizabeth Burns, *Theatricality* (London: Longman, 1972), pp. 31–3.
2. Mikhail Bakhtin, *The Dialogic Imagination* (trans. Caryl Emerson and Michael Holquist) (Austin: University of Texas, 1981), p. 34.
3. For an excellent discussion of the displacement of metaphorical language by metonymic devices on the naturalist stage, see Bert O. States, *Great Reckonings in Little Rooms: On the Phenomenology of Theater* (Berkeley: University of California Press, 1985), pp. 61–6.
4. John Orr, *Tragic Drama and Modern Society*, 2nd revised edn. (London: Macmillan, 1989), p. 3 ff., p. 50 ff.
5. *Signs Taken for Wonders* (London: Verso, 1988), p. 249 f.
6. Raymond Williams, *Drama from Ibsen to Brecht* (London: Oxford University Press, 1968), p. 334 f.
7. See the laudatory review of the 1928 New York Theater Guild production by Joseph Wood Krutch in Oscar Cargill (ed.), *O'Neill and His Plays: Four Decades of Criticism* (New York University Press, 1961), p. 184 f. A successful revival of the five-hour play, of what is at times an unreadable text, was directed in London by Keith Hacks in 1984. See John Orr, 'Thwarted Passion', in *Literary Review*, 73 (July 1984).
8. 'Modernisms', in B. Bergonzi (ed.), *Innovations* (London: Macmillan, 1968), p. 66 ff.

9.   *Aesthetic Theory* (trans. C. Lenhardt) (London: Routledge and Kegan Paul, 1984), pp. 34 f, 262 f.
10. Henri Bergson, *Matter and Memory* (trans. N. M. Paul and W. S. Palmer) (London: Macmillan, 1911), pp. 126–9. Significantly Gilles Deleuze uses Bergson's theory of recognitions to construct a model of time-images in the modernist film, consciously moving away from the semiology of his French predecessors to a perceptual theory of the cinematic form. See *Cinema 2: The Time Image* (trans. Hugh Tomlinson) (London: Athlone Press, 1989), pp. 45–9.
11. Roger Callois *Man, Play and Games* (trans. Meyer Barash) (New York: Free Press, 1961), pp. 11–37.
12. 'Homo Ludens Revisited', in Jacques Ehrmann (ed.), *Game, Play and Literature* (Boston: Beacon Press, 1968), p. 55.
13. Johan Huizinga, *Homo Ludens* (London: Routledge and Kegan Paul, 1949), Chapter 1.
14. See Fredric Jameson, 'Postmodernism and Consumer Society', in Hal Foster (ed.), *Postmodern Culture* (London: Pluto Press, 1985), p. 111 f.
15. *Role-Playing and Identity* (Bloomington: Indiana University Press, 1982), p. 38 f.
16. Ibid., p. 59.
17. It should also be remembered that Orson Welles, Ingmar Bergman and Andrej Wajda have been three of the most gifted theatre directors of the modern period. In his recent autobiography, Bergman acknowledges his debt as a film-maker to Scandinavian drama, and particularly Strindberg. See Ingmar Bergman, *The Magic Lantern* (trans. Joan Tate) (London: Hamish Hamilton, 1988).
18. Kermode, op. cit., p. 71.
19. *One-Dimensional Man* (Boston: Beacon Press, 1965), p. 49 f.
20. See Martin Walker, 'How Los Angeles was Lost', in *Guardian*, 2 September 1989; see also E. P. Thompson, 'Notes on Exterminism: The Last Stage of Civilisation', *New Left Review*, 121 (1980), pp. 3–27. On the visual derealisation effects of the new ballistic weapons systems see Paul Virilio, *War and Cinema: The Logistics of Perception* (trans. Patrick Camiller) (London: Verso, 1989), p. 84 f.
21. See the surveys analysed in Joe Bailey, *Pessimism* (London: Routledge and Kegan Paul, 1988), p. 40 ff.
22. *Writing and Society* (London: Verso, 1983), p. 17 f.
23. *The Culture of Narcissism* (London: Abacus, 1980), p. 71 ff.
24. Ibid., p. 125.

Chapter 3: The Resistance of Commodities

1.   *Modern Tragedy* (London: Verso, 1979) p. 87 ff.
2.   Charles Altieri, *Act and Quality* (Hassocks: Harvester, 1981, p. 308 ff.
3.   'Modernity and Revolution', *New Left Review*, 144 (1984), p. 113 f.
4.   *Blasting and Bombardiering* (London: Calder and Boyars, 1967), p. 207.
5.   Fredric Jameson, 'Postmodernism and Consumer Society', in Hal Foster (ed.), *Postmodern Culture* (London: Pluto Press, 1985), p. 114.

160 *Notes*

6. For the complex relationship between modernisms and modernity see Marshall Berman, *All That is Solid Melts into Air: The Experience of Modernity* (London: Verso, 1983); Ricardo Quinones, *Mapping Literary Modernism* (Princeton: Princeton University Press, 1985); Stephen Kern, *The Culture of Space and Time: 1880–1918* (London: Weidenfeld and Nicholson, 1983).

Chapter 4: Samuel Beckett: Imprisoned Persona and Irish Amnesia

1. 'Malone Dies', in *The Beckett Trilogy* (London: Picador, 1979), p. 168.
2. See the extensive analyses by Katherine Worth, *The Drama of Europe of Yeats to Beckett* (Atlantic Highlands, NJ: Humanities Press, 1974), Chapter 10, and D. E. S. Maxwell, *Modern Irish Drama: 1891–1980* (Cambridge: Cambridge University Press, 1984), Chapter 10.
3. *Collected Shorter Plays of Samuel Beckett* (London: Faber & Faber, 1984), p. 14.
4. Ibid., pp. 23–4.
5. *Being and Time* (Oxford: Basil Blackwell, 1962), p. 225 f.; see also George Steiner, *Heidegger* (London: Fontana, 1978), p. 94 f.
6. *Waiting for Godot* (London: Faber & Faber, 1959), p. 12.
7. Ibid., pp. 12–13.
8. Ibid., p. 22.
9. Ibid., p. 61.
10. Ibid., p. 88.
11. *Endgame* (London: Faber & Faber, 1958), p. 37.
12. Ibid., p. 26.

Chapter 5: Anglo-Tragic: Pinter and the English Tradition

1. Martin Esslin rightly stresses the sexual basis of Pinter's drama but his Freudian formulae are too reductive and untheatrical. See Martin Esslin, *Pinter: The Playwright* (London: Methuen, 1982). In criticising Esslin, however, Almansi and Henderson overbalance backwards into an equally reductive emphasis on language-games. See Guido Almansi and Simon Henderson, *Harold Pinter* (London: Methuen, 1983).
2. See David T. Thompson, *Pinter: The Player's Playwright* (London: Macmillan, 1985), p. 34 f.
3. 'The Dumb Waiter', in *Plays: One* (London: Methuen, 1986), p. 133.
4. Ibid., pp. 144, 162.
5. 'The Caretaker', in *Plays: Two* (London: Methuen, 1983), pp. 82–3.
6. Ibid., p. 40.

Chapter 6: Pinter: The Game of the Shared Experience

1. John Lahr (ed.), *The Orton Diaries* (London: Methuen, 1986), p. 238.
2. 'The Collection', in *Plays: Two* (London: Methuen, 1983), p. 155.
3. Ibid., p. 157.
4. 'The Lover', in *Plays: Two* (London: Methuen, 1983), p. 170.

5. Ibid., p. 183.
6. 'The Homecoming', in *Plays: Three* (London: Methuen, 1978), pp. 49–50.
7. Ibid., p. 65.
8. Ibid., p. 63.
9. Ibid., p. 69.

Chapter 7: Shepard I: The Rise of Myth/The Fall of Community

1. *Acting Out America* (Harmondsworth: Penguin, 1972), p. 173 f.
2. See Shepard's own introduction to *The Unseen Hand* where he refers to the junk towns of Southern California in which he had spent his youth. *Action and The Unseen Hand* (London: Faber & Faber, 1975), pp. 47–8.
3. 'Icarus's Mother', in *Chicago and Other Plays* (New York: Applause Theater Book Publishers, 1981), pp. 35–6.
4. Ibid., pp. 38–9.
5. Ibid., p. 55.
6. Ibid., p. 57.
7. *Chicago and Other Plays* contains directors' accounts of working on productions of Shepard's plays; Ralph Cook on *Chicago*, Sydney Schubart Walter on *Fourteen Hundred Thousand*, Michael Smith on *Icarus's Mother* and Jacques Levy on *Red Cross*. Schechner's account of his work on *The Tooth of Crime* can be found in *Environmental Theater* (New York: Hawthornden Books, 1973).
8. Ellen Oumana, *Sam Shepard* (London: Virgin, 1987), p. 51.
9. 'The Tooth of Crime', in *Sam Shepard: Seven Plays* (London: Faber, 1985), p. 203.
10. Ibid., p. 216–17.
11. Ibid., p. 219.
12. Ibid., pp.229–30.
13. Schechner, op. cit., pp. 235–6.
14. *Action and The Unseen Hand* (London: Faber, 1975), p. 27.
15. Ibid., p. 29.

Chapter 8: Shepard II: The Shock of the Normal

1. 'Curse of the Starving Class', in *Sam Shepard: Seven Plays* (London: Faber, 1985), p. 139.
2. Ibid., p. 150.
3. Ibid., p. 157.
4. Ibid., p. 156.
5. Ibid., p. 200.
6. 'Buried Child', in *Sam Shepard: Seven Plays* (London: Faber, 1985), pp. 110–11.

Chapter 9: Shepard III: Re-Enacting the Myth of Origin

1. *Indians* (London: Methuen, 1970), p. 69.

Bibliography

Plays

Albee, Edward. *The Zoo Story and the American Dream: Two Plays*. New York: Signet, 1971.
    The Sandbox and The Death of Bessie Smith. New York: Signet, 1963.
    Who's Afraid Of Virginia Woolf? Harmondsworth: Penguin, 1970.
Beckett, Samuel. *Waiting for Godot*. London: Faber & Faber, 1959.
    Endgame. London: Faber & Faber, 1958.
    Collected Shorter Plays. London: Faber & Faber, 1984.
Bond, Edward. *Plays*, Vols 1–3. London: Methuen, 1978–9.
Bullins, Ed. 'The Electronic Nigger', in *New American Plays*, Vol. 3. New York: Hill and Wang, 1970.
Gelber, Jack. *The Connection*. London: Faber & Faber, 1960.
Genet, Jean. *Deathwatch*. London: Faber & Faber, 1977.
    The Maids. London: Faber & Faber, 1978.
    The Balcony (revised version). London: Faber & Faber, 1978.
    The Blacks. London: Faber & Faber, 1973.
Guare, John. *The House of Blue Leaves*. New York: Plume, 1987.
Hampton, Christopher. *The Philanthropist*. London: Faber & Faber, 1971.
    Savages. London: Faber & Faber, 1974.
    Les Liaisons Dangereuses. London: Faber & Faber, 1985.
Hare, David. *The Secret Rapture*. London: Faber & Faber, 1988.
Kopit, Arthur. *Indians*. London: Methuen, 1970.
    End of the World. New York: Hill and Wang, 1984.
Mamet, David. *American Buffalo*. London: Methuen, 1978.
    Glengarry Glen Ross. London: Methuen, 1984.
    Speed-The Plow. London: Methuen, 1988.
O'Neill, Eugene. *The Plays of Eugene O'Neill*, 3 vols. New York: Random House, 1954.
    Long Day's Journey into Night. London: Cape, 1976.
Orton, Joe. *The Complete Plays*. London: Methuen, 1976.
Pinter, Harold. *Plays*, Vols 1–4. London: Methuen, 1978–83.
    One For the Road. London: Methuen, 1984.
    Mountain Language. London: Faber & Faber, 1988.
Pirandello, Luigi. *Collected Plays*, Vols 1 and 2. London: John Calder, 1987–8.
Shepard, Sam. *Chicago and Other Plays*. New York: Applause Theater Publishers, 1981.
    Four Two-Act Plays. London: Faber & Faber, 1981.
    Action and The Unseen Hand. London: Faber & Faber, 1975.
    Seven Plays. London: Faber & Faber, 1985.
    Fool for Love. London: Faber & Faber, 1985.
    A Lie of the Mind. London: Methuen, 1986.
Soyinka, Wole. *Collected Plays*, Vol. 1. Oxford: Oxford University Press, 1973.

A Play of Giants. London: Methuen, 1984.
Synge J. M. *Collected Works*, 4 Vols. London: Oxford University Press, 1966.
Yeats, W. B. *The Collected Plays of W. B. Yeats*, London: Macmillan, 1954.

Select Critical Bibliography

Adorno, Theodor, *Noten zur Literatur*, Vols I–III. Frankfurt: Suhrkampf, 1958, 1961, 1963.
    Aesthetic Theory (trans. C. Lenhardt). London: Routledge and Kegan Paul, 1984.
    'Towards an Understanding of Endgame', in Bell Gale Chevigny (ed.), *Twentieth Century Interpretations of Endgame*. Englewood Cliffs, NJ: Prentice Hall, 1989.
Almansi, Guido and Henderson, Simon. *Harold Pinter*. London: Methuen, 1983.
Altieri, Charles. *Act and Quality*. Hassocks: Harvester, 1981.
Alvarez, A. *Beckett*. London: Fontana, 1971.
Anderson, Perry. 'Modernity and Revolution', *New Left Review*, 144 (March–April 1984).
Artaud, Antonin. *The Theatre and Its Double* (trans. Mary Caroline Richards). New York: Grove Press, 1958.
Bailey, Joe. *Pessimism*. London: Routledge and Kegan Paul, 1988.
Bakhtin, Mikhail. *The Dialogic Imagination* (trans. Caryl Emerson and Michael Holquist). Austin: University of Texas, 1981.
Bergson, Henri, *Matter and Memory* (trans. Nancy Margaret Paul and W. Scott Palmer). London: Macmillan, 1911.
Berman, Marshall *All that is Solid Melts into Air: The Experience of Modernity* London: Verso, 1983.
Bigsby, C. W. *Twentieth Century American Drama*, Vols I–III. Cambridge: Cambridge University Press, 1985.
Bogard, Travis. *Contour in Time: The Plays of Eugene O'Neill*, 2nd edn. Oxford: Oxford University Press, 1988.
Brook, Peter. *The Empty Space*. Harmondsworth: Penguin, 1980.
Brustein, Robert. *The Theatre of Revolt*. London: Methuen, 1965.
Burns, Elizabeth, *Theatricality*. London: Longman, 1972.
Caillois, Roger. *Man, Play and Games* (trans. Meyer Barash). New York: Free Press, 1961.
Carmier, Ramona and Pallister, Janis L. *Waiting for Death: The Philosophical Significance of Beckett's En Attendant Godot*. Alabama: University of Alabama Press, 1980.
Cetta, Lewis T. *Profane Play, Ritual and Jean Genet*. Alabama: University of Alabama Press, 1974.
Cohn, Ruby. *Samuel Beckett: The Comic Gamut*. New Brunswick: Rutgers University Press, 1962.
    Just Play: Beckett's Theatre (Princeton: Princeton University Press, 1980.
    New American Dramatists: 1960–1980. London: Macmillan, 1982.
Deleuze, Gilles. *Cinema 2: The Time Image* (trans. Hugh Tomlinson and Robert Galeta). London: Athlone Press, 1989.
Derrida, Jacques. *Glas*. Paris: Editions Galilée, 1974.

Dukore, Bernard. *When Laughter Stops: Pinter's Tragicomedy.* Columbia: University of Missouri Press, 1976.

Dutton, Richard. *Tragicomedy and the British Tradition.* Hassocks: Harvester, 1986.

Ehrmann, Jacques (ed.). *Game, Play and Literature.* Boston: Beacon Press, 1968.

Eigen, Manfred and Winkler, Ruthild. *Laws of the Game: How the Principles of Nature Govern Chance* (trans. Robert and Rita Kember). Harmondsworth: Penguin, 1983.

Esslin, Martin. *The Theatre of the Absurd*, revised edn. Harmondsworth: Penguin, 1968.

   Pinter: The Playwright, 4th revised edn. London: Methuen, 1982.

Gerould, Daniel (ed.). *American Melodrama.* New York: PAJ Publications, 1983.

Goffman, Erving. *The Presentation of Self in Everyday Life.* Harmondsworth: Penguin, 1969.

   Frame Analysis: An Essay on the Organisation of Experience. New York: Harper and Row, 1974.

Haug, W. F. *Critique of Commodity Aesthetics: Appearance, Sexuality and Advertising in Capitalist Society* (trans. Robert Bock). Cambridge: Polity Press, 1986.

Heidegger, Martin. *Being and Time* (trans. J. Macquarrie and E. Robinson). Oxford: Basil Blackwell, 1962.

Huizinga, Johann. *Homo Ludens.* London: Routledge and Kegan Paul, 1949.

Jameson, Fredric. 'Postmodernism and Consumer Society', in Hal Foster (ed.), *Postmodern Culture.* London: Pluto Press, 1985.

Kermode, Frank. 'Modernisms', in Bernard Bergonzi (ed.), *Innovations.* London: Macmillan, 1968.

Knowles, Bernard. 'The Caretaker and the "Point of Laughter" ', *Journal of Beckett Studies* (Autumn 1979).

Krutch, Joseph Wood. 'Strange Interlude', in Oscar Cargill (ed.) *O'Neill and His Plays: Four Decades of Criticism.* New York: New York University Press, 1961.

Lahr, John. *Acting out America: Essays in the American Theatre.* Harmondsworth: Penguin, 1972.

   The Orton Diaries. London: Methuen, 1986.

Lasch, Christopher. *The Culture of Narcissism.* London: Abacus, 1980.

Lewis, Wyndham. *Blasting and Bombardiering.* London: Calder and Boyars, 1967.

Marcuse, Herbert. *One-Dimensional Man.* Boston: Beacon Press, 1968.

Maxwell, D. E. S. *A Critical History of Modern Irish Drama: 1891–1980.* Cambridge: Cambridge University Press, 1984.

Moretti, Franco. *Signs Taken for Wonders*, 2nd revised edn. London: Verso, 1988.

Morranca, Bonnie (ed.). *American Dreams: The Imagination of Sam Shepard.* New York: PAJ Publications, 1981.

Morrison, Kristin. *Cantors and Chronicles: The Use of Narrative in the Plays of Samuel Beckett and Harold Pinter.* Chicago: University of Chicago Press, 1983.

Orr, John. *Tragic Drama and Modern Society*, 2nd revised edn. London: Macmillan, 1989.

Oumano, Ellen. *Sam Shepard: The Life and Work of an American Dreamer*. London: Virgin, 1987.

Peter, John. *Vladimir's Carrot: Modern Drama and the Modern Imagination*. London: Methuen, 1988.

Quigley, Austin. *The Pinter Problem*. Princeton, NJ: Princeton University Press, 1975.

    The Modern Stage and Other Worlds. London: Methuen, 1985.

Sartre, Jean-Paul. *Being and Nothingness* (trans. Hazel Barnes). London: Methuen, 1957.

    Saint-Genet: Actor and Martyr (trans. Bernard Frechtmann). New York: Signet Classics, 1970.

Savona, Jeanette L. *Jean Genet*. London: Macmillan, 1983.

Schechner, Richard. *Experimental Theatre*. New York: Hawthorne Books, 1973.

Scheaffer, Louis. *O'Neill: Son and Artist*. London: Dent, 1974.

Sloterdijk, Peter. *Critique of Cynical Reason* (trans. Michael Eldred). London: Verso, 1988.

States, Bert O. *The Shape of Paradox*. Berkeley: University of California Press, 1978.

    Great Reckonings in Little Rooms: On the Phenomenology of Theatre. Berkeley: University of California Press, 1985.

Steiner, George. *Heidegger*. London: Fontana, 1978.

Stevenson, Randall. 'Harold Pinter – Innovator?', in Alan Bold (ed.), *Harold Pinter*. London: Vision Press, 1984.

Szondi, Peter. *Theory of the Modern Drama* (trans. Michael Hays). Cambridge: Polity Press, 1986.

Thompson, David T. *Pinter: The Player's Playwright*. London: Macmillan, 1985.

Virilio, Paul. *War and Cinema: The Logistics of Perception* (trans. Patrick Camiller). London: Verso, 1989.

Williams, Raymond. *The Long Revolution*. Harmondsworth: Penguin, 1963.

    Drama from Ibsen to Brecht. Harmondsworth: Penguin, 1986.

    Marxism and Literature. Oxford: Oxford University Press, 1977.

    Politics and Letters. London: Verso, 1978.

    Modern Tragedy, 2nd revised edn. London: Verso, 1979.

    Writing in Society. London: Verso, 1983.

    The Politics of Modernism (ed. and intro. by Tony Pinckney). London: Verso, 1989.

Wilshire, Bruce. *Role-Playing and Identity*. Bloomington: Indiana University Press, 1982.

Worth, Katherine. *The Irish Drama of Europe from Yeats to Beckett*. Atlantic Highlands, NJ: Humanities Press, 1978.

Index

Adorno, Theodor, 4, 6, 17
advertising, 6–8, 29–30
Albee, Edward, 14, 23, 32, 148–9,
  151; *Tiny Alice*, 32; *Who's Afraid of
  Virginia Woolf?*, 20, 23; *The Zoo
  Story*, 32, 148–9, 151
Almansi, Guido, 160n.
Altman, Robert, 147
Anderson, Perry, 42, 45
Antonioni, Michaelangelo, 24, 45
apocalypse, 5, 9, 25ff., 62–5, 110–
  11, 127f.
Arden, John, 46, 70
Artaud, Antonin, 5
auteurs, 24

Bakhtin, Mikhail, 11, 63
Barthes, Roland, 6, 63
Baudrillard, Jean, 6
Beckett, Samuel, 1, 2, 4–5, 9, 14, 17,
  19–22, 27, 32, 34, 35, 41, 42, 46,
  47–71, 72, 75, 81, 82, 93, 105, 113,
  118–19, 120, 124, 125, 127, 130,
  135, 136, 139; *All that Fall*, 50–2,
  64–5; *Catastrophe*, 69–70, 81;
  Endgame, 21, 30, 34, 37, 38, 51, 56,
  61–6, 69–70, 92, 98, 118–19, 127,
  128, 141, 143–4; *Footfalls*, 68;
  Happy Days, 51, 68; *Krapp's Last
  Tape*, 66–8; *Malone Dies*, 47–8;
  Molloy, 47–8; *Murphy*, 47; *Not I*,
  68; *Ohio Impromptu*, 68; *Play*, 68;
  Rockaby, 68; *Waiting for Godot*, 1,
  10, 14, 19, 21–2, 27, 32, 35, 37, 38,
  40, 47, 49–50, 51, 52–61, 80, 82;
  Watt, 47
Bergson, Henri, 17
Bergman, Ingmar, 24, 25
Bertolucci, Bernardo, 24
bisexuality, 88ff., 149
Blake, William, 58
Bond, Edward, 14, 20, 32, 46, 72,
  73, 82, 139; *Saved*, 10, 20, 32, 46,
  72, 73, 82, 139; *The Sea*, 32

Brecht, Bertolt, 3–4, 9, 14, 17, 34,
  45, 46, 52, 129, 130, 153
Brenton, Howard, 46; *The Romans
  in Britain*, 10
Bresson, Robert, 45
Brown, Norman O., 112
Buntline, Ned, 146
Buñuel, Luis, 24

Caillois, Roger, 18
Camus, Albert, 52; *Caligula*, 52;
  Requiem for a Nun, 52
Chekhov, Anton, 3, 11, 12, 16, 17,
  24, 36–7, 72; *The Seagull*, 11; *Three
  Sisters*, 36
Christianity, 52ff.
Chaikin, Joe, 117
citizenship, 23, 40–1
Cluchey, Rick, 61
Cody, Buffalo Bill, 145–6
Cohn, Ruby, 4
cold war, 43f.
commodifications, 5–6, 17, 29–30,
  37, 41ff., 134f., 146f.
communalism, 118ff.
consumerism, 6–9, 26ff., 43–4, 134f.
Cook, Ralph, 117
Coppola, Francis Ford, 110;
  Apocalypse Now, 110, 112
counter-culture, 29f., 110–12, 124ff.
Critical Theory, 4, 8, 25

Dean, James, 44
Deleuze, Gilles, 6, 159n.
Descartes, René, 53
Dickens, Charles, 85
disrecognitions, 2, 8–9, 17–19, 25,
  30, 32, 33ff., 41, 45, 48–9, 133f.
drugs culture, 36, 110–12, 114–16,
  119–23, 124ff.
Dürrenmatt, Friedrich, 46

Eastwood, Clint, 119; *High Plains
  Drifter*, 119

166